"DRIVE illustrates the five buying personalities. The good news is you already speak one. The bad news is you're accidentally alienating the other four which is costing you sales. Learn the missing four buying personalities and you have the potential to increase your sales by 400%."

*Garrett Gunderson*
*New York Times Bestselling Author of Killing Sacred Cows*

"After I trained with Woody I cleared six figures on my first keynote speech by implementing DRIVE. This system will forever change your sales."

*Ron Williams*
*7-time Mr. Natural Olympia*
*7-time Mr. Natural Universe*
*7-time Mr. Natural World*

"At JetBlue I taught my team how to use DRIVE to resolve customer concerns, lower employee turnover, and increase team morale. DRIVE is my go-to system to increase customer engagement."

*Anna Smith*
*JetBlue Senior CSVC*

"I invited Woody to speak at one of my international events. I challenged him to use DRIVE to sell one of MY products, not his. When the final numbers came in, he increased my sales by 1440%. If you want to change your sales numbers read this book."

*Rob Sperry*
*The Game of Networking*

"The DRIVE Sales System has helped us raise $2,386,400 in capital for investments. When you are negotiating terms, knowing the DRIVE of the person sitting across the table from you is a game-changer."

*Daniel and Sam Kwak*
*Investors*

"Since being introduced to DRIVE my philosophy of business management and entrepreneurship has changed significantly. DRIVE centered strategies and business plans produce results! It takes the 'guessing' out of sales, marketing, and managing staff."

*Matthew Casto*
*Senior Art Director, Universal Studios*

"In three years, I took my company from my garage to being one of Inc 500's Fastest Growing Companies. Woody has been my business strategist for over 10 years, and I attribute so much of my success, both personally and financially, to his brilliant DRIVE program."

*Inger Erickson*
*Uppercase Living*

"I had the honor of having Woody perform the true power of DRIVE in front of a live audience at an event I ran in Australia. It was so powerful the audience demanded additional training. We had to change the agenda to make room for him to dive deeper. It was one of the most relevant and mind-blowing trainings I have ever witnessed."

*Frazer Brookes*
*Social Media Strategist*

"If you are a mind reader, you do NOT need this book. But if by chance you find yourself lacking in mind-reading skills—activate the DRIVE Sales System immediately. It will give you laser focus on closing more sales and increasing your income."

*Troy Dunn*
*TV Host*

"DRIVE not only increased my business and our non-profit, it has enlightened us to know how to empower others! DRIVE took us to the next level!"

*Leesa Price*
*CEO Princess Warrior*

"IT WORKS! We have grown our business by almost 100% since implementing the DRIVE Sales System."

*Eric Counts*
*Founder of CreditNerds.com*

"When I first met Woody I was already successful but lost in my own world. Through his DRIVE system I learned how to create myself as an asset and how to start attracting all the right people and situations into my life. With his help my life took off and I've been able to create a life I never dreamed of before. This book is a must-read, more so for one's self but also for their business."

*Jimmy Rex*
*You End Up Where You're Heading*

"DRIVE has taken my sales to the next level by helping me understand how to identify the five buying personality types. If you are looking to increase your sales and gain a new mindset, skillset, and toolset—this book delivers."

*Cody Hofhine*
*Co-Founder Wholesaling Inc.*

"Woody is one of the most creative people I've ever met. He has the ability to break complex subjects into simple, step by step concepts. This is what he has done with sales in DRIVE. If you want to sell more, and if you want to know why your prospects are buying from you, then you need DRIVE."

*Justin Prince*
*Change Your World*

"You cannot make a difference in the lives of others until you know what DRIVEs them. Being able to connect on a deep intimate level will allow you to create wealth in your life, relationships, and in your business."

*Greg S. Reid*
*Think and Grow Rich; Three Feet from Gold*

"DRIVE is a wonderful tool I highly recommend for you to discover who you really are, which will allow you to have more love, wealth, health, and joy in your life."

*Jack Canfield*
*New York Times Bestselling Co-Author of Chicken Soup for the Soul*

"As you begin to understand your DRIVE and gain insight into yourself, it gives you a greater insight into others, and insight allows you to make a greater impact in life."

*Les Brown*
*Laws of Success*

"When you are marketing to someone, you must understand their DRIVE to trigger their buying buttons. Woody Woodward will teach you how to discover your customer's DRIVE and what causes them to buy more."

*Joel Comm*
*New York Times Bestselling Author of Twitter Power*

# D.R.I.V.E.
# SALES

**Other Books by Woody Woodward**

*Your Emotional Fingerprint—7 Secrets That Will Transform Your Life*

*Millionaire Dropouts—Inspiring Stories of the World's Greatest Failures*

*Millionaire Dropouts—Biography Edition*

*Millionaire Dropouts—High School Edition*

*Millionaire Dropouts—Words of Wisdom*

*Millionaire Dropouts—Innovators*

*B.S. And Other Advice About Money*

*Parables For Profit Vol. 1*

*Parables For Profit Vol. 2*

*Parables For Profit Vol. 3*

# D.R.I.V.E. SALES

## The 5 Secrets to Increase Sales by 400%

Woody Woodward

RENEGADE
PUBLISHING

The following Trademarks are registered by Woody Woodward
DRIVE Sales System™
DRIVE Assessment™
Discover Your Drive™



For bulk orders www.DRIVESalesBook.com/Contact

**Warning—Disclaimer**
The purpose of this book is to educate and inspire. It is not intended to give advice, make promises, or guarantees that anyone following the ideas, tips, suggestions, techniques, or strategies will have the same results as the people listed throughout the stories contained herein. The author, publisher, and distributor(s) shall have neither liability nor responsibility to anyone with respect to any loss or damage caused, or alleged to be caused, directly or indirectly, by the information. The author has used interviews, biographies, and documentaries to give the best educated guess on all the individuals' DRIVE referenced in this book. No guarantees are implied or granted.

ISBN 978-0-9982340-6-9
Printed in the United States of America

For Bob Snyder, who gave me the greatest advice ever: "Don't Be Stupid! You are not done developing DRIVE. Keep going." Without his encouragement and wise counsel this book would never have been.

To all my clients and the thousands of conversations around DRIVE, this book is because of you. Without your commitment to build your business and revolutionize your relationships, I would not have any of this content. May you have a sense of pride in this work as you see our conversations and discoveries unfold on these pages.

To my dear wife and kids. You have sacrificed the most. There are no worldly accolades or successes that will ever compensate for your sacrifice. Without you and your support none of this would exist.

# Contents

# Introduction

You lose eighty percent of your sales by opening your mouth.

Two friends drove past the city limits on a dirt road leading to open fields dotted with horses and orchards. Walter pulled the car to the side of the road and vividly described to his friend what he was going to build on this desolate land. He wanted to convince his friend Arthur to buy all the surrounding acreage.

Walter told Arthur, "I can handle the main project myself. It will take all my money, but I want you to have the first chance at this surrounding acreage. In the next five years, it will increase in value several times."

Arthur looked around and thought to himself, *Who in the world is going to drive twenty-five miles for this crazy project? His dream has gotten the best of his common sense.* Arthur gave Walter all the excuses a good friend could give while trying not to squash the other's dream.

But Walter implored Arthur to buy the remaining land. Arthur refused to concede. Money was a little tight, he said, and now was not the best time to invest. But he would think about it and get back to Walter later.

"Later on will be too late," cautioned Walter. "You better move on it right now."

Art Linkletter failed to see the vision of his close friend Walt Disney. One year later, on July 17, 1955, Walt opened Disneyland and Art was the Master of Ceremonies. Linkletter had missed an opportunity of a lifetime by failing to purchase the land surrounding one of today's most well-known amusement parks: Disneyland.

While Arthur had failed to see the vision of his close friend, someone else hadn't. In 1954, the year Disney was building his dream, the Fujishige family purchased fifty-six acres of strawberry fields across the street for $2,500. In the late 1990s, the Disney Corporation paid the family just under $100 million for the land. Whose fault was it that Linkletter didn't see the opportunity? Was it Disney's—or Linkletter's?

"I will sell you ten percent of the Denver Broncos for $15 million." That was the offer Broncos owner Pat Bowlen offered to star quarterback John Elway before the 1998 NFL season. Bowlen also offered to throw in another ten percent of the franchise on one condition: Elway would have to defer the salary he was owed—about $21 million—and become a personal assistant to Bowlen, which would eventually lead to him becoming chief operating officer.

By itself, that doesn't seem like a terrible deal: twenty percent ownership of an NFL franchise for $36 million. Bowlen sweetened the deal even further: if Elway became unsatisfied with his investment, Bowlen would refund his money two to five years later, plus give him an additional $5 million, and eight percent interest per year. Elway had nothing to lose; the Broncos would guarantee his investment.

Elway could have easily afforded the investment. Just a year earlier, he had sold his car dealerships for $82.5 million. It was the largest off-the-field business deal an NFL player had ever made.

Elway had nine months to think about the offer. In January 1999, he led the Broncos to their second straight Super Bowl victory. That May, he retired after sixteen seasons in the league. Unfortunately, he did not invest in the team. Instead, he put money into a sports tech stock and a Ponzi scheme, losing more than $36 million.

Today, the Broncos are worth $2.7 billion. A twenty percent stake would be worth $540 million, which would have given him a 1,500 percent ROI. So, whose fault was it he did not invest? Was it owner Pat Bowlen's or John Elway's?

There is one reason why our pitches fall flat. We are not speaking our potential customer's buying language. The business graveyard is littered with the lost opportunities of individuals who could not convey their message to make a deal.

Consider the following:

- Nolan Bushnell, founder of Atari, was Steve Jobs' first boss. Jobs offered Bushnell one-third of Apple for $50,000. Bushnell was unconvinced and passed on the investment. Why?
- Billionaire Ross Perot could have owned a majority of Microsoft in 1979 for $60 million. But he never pulled the trigger. A majority of Microsoft today would be worth $512 billion—an 850,000 percent ROI. Why did he not see the value?
- Myspace CEO Chris DeWolfe was offered Facebook for $75 million by Mark Zuckerberg, but he passed. Why did DeWolfe not see the full potential of Facebook?

- In 1999, Excite could have bought Google for $750,000. Two years later, Excite filed for bankruptcy. What went wrong?
- Decca Records passed on the Beatles. The Beatles went on to become one of the biggest rock and roll bands in history. How did Decca miss that opportunity?
- Western Union was offered the telephone from inventor Alexander Graham Bell for $100,000 and passed. Why did they not see the potential?
- In 2006, Yahoo! shook hands with Mark Zuckerberg to purchase Facebook for $1 billion—and then backed out. What caused them to back out? In 2016, Verizon purchased a collapsing Yahoo! for $4.6 billion. And Facebook is now worth $538 billion.

There are five buying personalities that DRIVE sales: Directors, Relators, Intellectuals, Validators, and Executives. You pitch based on *your* own DRIVE, which means you do not effectively sell to the other eighty percent. The good news, though, is that the easiest sale you will ever make is to someone with the same DRIVE.

Here is what you will learn through the DRIVE Sales System™:

- How to sell to each DRIVE, thus potentially increasing your sales by 400 percent
- How to capitalize on your own DRIVE to increase your revenue
- How to prepare your offer for maximum impact using DRIVE
- How to use a *reassociation* to create buying behavior
- How to close the sale with "ASK. Don't Tell."
- How to close the sale with "SHOW. Don't Tell."
- How to save the sale with PICKS

Before you get the keys to the sales kingdom and are set loose with these new techniques, you need to understand your personal DRIVE System—why you buy and what motivates you—so you can be prepared to craft the proper pitch to your potential customers. Once you do, you'll be able to dramatically increase your sales.

1

# The DRIVE Assessment

"I know what you are doing, but it doesn't feel like you are selling me; it feels like a conversation." Alex Glaittli had just used the DRIVE Sales System™ for the first time. He had been speaking to a potential client for ten months and had made no progress. After understanding the principles of DRIVE, he was able to speak his client's buying language and closed the deal.

Ernő Rubik invented one of the most popular three-dimensional puzzles in history. His Rubik's Cube is undoubtedly one of the most well-known toys in the world, with over 350 million units sold. This simple three-inch cube has over forty-three quintillion combinations (43,252,003,274,489,856,000, to be precise). Despite its incredible complexity, it can be solved using seven key algorithms, or seven specific steps. In fact, in 2018, thirteen-year-old Yusheng Du set the world record for solving it in 3.47 seconds.

Just like the Rubik's Cube, every human personality has myriad facets, moods, preferences, opinions, and habits. There is, however, a simple algorithm that explains why we buy and why we do what we do. It is called DRIVE. Rubik's three-inch cube has seven steps to solving the quintillion options, and your DRIVE consists of a mere seven characteristics that move your behavior.

## DRIVE Assessment Instructions

**Step 1.** Read the seven words on each of the D.R.I.V.E. cards.

**Step 2.** Read through them again and rank The D.R.I.V.E. Cards based on the card with the most words that make you feel important, not what is important to you. This is critical in properly identifying your DRIVE. There are things that are important to you, like work or family, but those items may not make you feel important. Choose the one group that makes you feel important. If you get stuck between two groups, ask yourself, "Which one could I not live without?"

**Example:** R, E, D, I, V

# What Makes You *Feel* Important?

## Ⓓ

- Experiencing Life
- Life's Purpose
- Freedom
- Creativity
- Performing
- Overcoming
- Appearance

## Ⓡ

- Relationships
- Influence
- Service
- Family
- Friends
- Parent
- Spirituality

## Ⓘ

- Knowledge
- Learning
- Health
- Nature
- Moment
- Standards
- Organized

## Ⓥ

- Recognition
- Accepted
- Praise
- Trust
- Respect
- Validation
- Being Needed

## Ⓔ

- Winning
- Control
- Work
- Goals
- Security
- Providing
- Problem Solving

Below is a snapshot of the DRIVE personalities. In the next chapter, we will go into greater detail about each one. If you felt torn between two groups during the assessment, don't worry—that will be covered in Chapter 4: The Why vs. How.

- Group D is a Director (p. 11)
- Group R is a Relator (p. 13)
- Group I is an Intellectual (p. 15)
- Group V is a Validator (p. 17)
- Group E is an Executive (p. 19)

For now, read **only** about your DRIVE. Come back later to review the other four DRIVEs when you choose to market to them.

## DIRECTOR

D

A Director loves to feel free and independent, has a purpose for what they do, and thrives on experiencing life. They enjoy being creative and discovering new things. Directors are innovators, performers, orchestrators, and collaborators; they can take an immense amount of diverse information and synthesize it into information easily grasped by the masses. They are great in social settings and in bringing people together to make something happen. They find joy in overcoming obstacles and making a difference in the world.

### *Strengths*

- Creative, outgoing, and passionate about what they do
- Spontaneous and adventurous in the way they approach life
- Expressive, fashionable, stylish, and confident
- Don't give up and are eternally optimistic
- Can be strong-willed and will not allow themselves to be pushed around
- Have a clear vision of what they want and are willing to sacrifice for that purpose
- Open-minded and think outside the box

### *Weaknesses*

- Sometimes unsympathetic with those who complain
- Hard on themselves about their appearance
- Can be a non-team player and at times isolate
- Frustrated when people do not value their creativity
- Disappointed when they are not achieving their life's purpose
- Others cannot keep up with their impulsiveness and spontaneity
- Can get exhausted from always trying to do everything

### *Buying Motivators*

Directors are motivated to create their ideal *Lifestyle.* When purchasing a product or service, they want to know how it is going to enhance their lifestyle or give them the life they want. They are attracted to products or services that will help them achieve financial freedom, time freedom, or give them a VIP experience.

### *Examples of Successful Directors*

- Walt Disney (Disney)
- Sir Richard Branson (the Virgin Group)
- J. K. Rowling (Author—Harry Potter Series)
- Nick Woodman (GoPro)
- Ferruccio Lamborghini (Lamborghini)
- Sara Blakely (Spanx)
- Theodore Geisel (Dr. Seuss)
- Elon Musk (Tesla, SpaceX)

## RELATOR

(R)

Relators find value in building strong, healthy, long-term relationships. Relationships are both important to them and make them feel important. In the workforce, their strength is in networking and building other people up to a higher level of productivity and accountability. If their relationships are struggling, they feel challenged to be productive. Relators garner energy and security through their relationships. They are loyal to their friends, enjoy having the power of influence, strive to be good parents, and are service-minded. They desire to see their relationships continue to deepen and grow.

### *Strengths*

- Compassionate, loving, and caring in relationships
- Charitable, forgiving, and a peacemaker
- Easy to talk to and a great listener
- Puts the team, family, or friends before their own needs
- Feels secure in their relationships
- Natural team leader
- Often will be the first to raise their hand to volunteer

### *Weaknesses*

- Serves and sacrifices too much, often to their detriment
- Can exhaust themselves by giving too much to everyone else
- Takes on another person's work instead of saying "no"
- Tends to not stand up for themselves during confrontations
- Often will not share their real opinion for fear of offending you
- Can be overly empathetic, taking on others' sadness or depression

### *Buying Motivators*

Relators are motivated by *Community*. When purchasing a product or service, they tend to consult with family, friends, or their extended social community before making a decision. They are driven to invest in their community and are more inclined to affiliate with or purchase products that give back.

### *Examples of Successful Relators*

- Oprah Winfrey (OWN Network)
- Amadeo Giannini (Founder, Bank of America)
- Jimmy Fallon (The Tonight Show host)
- Rosa Parks (Civil Rights Activist)
- Bono (lead singer of U2)
- Bob Iger (former CEO, Disney Corp.)
- Milton Hershey (Hershey Chocolates)
- Mother Teresa (Caregiver)
- Joe Gebbia Jr. (Cofounder, Airbnb)

## INTELLECTUAL

I

Intellectuals are stimulated through books, speeches, research, reading, conversations, nature, or organization. They feel successful when accomplishing a task. They are motivated to learn, grow, and be healthy. They would rather be learning something new than just lying around. They want to better themselves and become more useful. They are driven to understand and to be more knowledgeable. They like to share what they know with others.

### *Strengths*

- Task and goal-oriented
- Health-conscious, striving to eat healthy and be physically fit
- Intelligent and stimulated by new knowledge
- Strives to take care of the planet
- Bright, curious, and inquisitive
- Great at building systems
- Can follow step-by-step processes

### *Weaknesses*

- Struggles with analysis paralysis
- Prone to overthinking a problem or situation
- Does not appreciate advice from others
- Feels as if they are the smartest person in the room
- Can be judgmental of others who cannot keep pace intellectually
- Can be a know-it-all
- Often gets frustrated when someone changes their schedule or is late

### *Buying Motivators*

Intellectuals are motivated by *Systems*. When purchasing a product or service, they are looking for the details or step-by-step actions they need to take to achieve the desired goal. They want to enhance their intelligence and expertise. They desire to share what they know with others.

### *Examples of Successful Intellectuals*

- Michelle Obama (Former U.S. 1st Lady)
- Warren Buffet (Berkshire Hathaway)
- Arianna Huffington (Huffington Post)
- Jeff Bezos (Amazon)
- Michael Dell (Dell Computers)
- Florence Nightingale (Social Reformer)
- Will Kellogg (Kellogg)
- Sheryl Sandberg (Facebook COO)
- James Dyson (Dyson)
- Ingvar Kamprad (IKEA)
- Ray Kroc (McDonald's)

## VALIDATOR

V

Validators feel important when they are being trusted, respected, praised, recognized, accepted, or needed. They enjoy small, intimate groups of people where they are being validated. They are often wonderful at giving validation to others. They do not like to be ignored, and they are offended when people they care about disrespect them. Validators' confidence stems from the strength of their relationships. If they feel like they are in a healthy, caring, and trusted relationship, they feel strong, secure, and loved.

### *Strengths*

- Great at validating others
- The team motivator and cheerleader
- Strives to be trustworthy
- Respectful of others' opinions and desires
- Thrives in small, intimate social groups and settings
- Can be a team player and will support others' opinions

### *Weaknesses*

- Does not like to be ignored
- Frustrated when people do not validate their opinion or input
- Can be needy at times
- Disappointed when people don't need them
- Can be over-trusting and be taken advantage of
- Can be jealous of others' success or accolades

### *Buying Motivators*

Validators are motivated by giving and receiving *Admiration*. When purchasing a product or service, they are driven to use it to help others, or to help them be a better leader that people want to follow. If they buy, they want to know how it will make them look better to their peers, friends, or family.

### *Examples of Successful Validators*

- Mark Cuban (Shark Tank)
- Ellen DeGeneres (Comedian - TV host)
- Art Linkletter (Radio and TV host)
- Mick Jagger (Rolling Stones)
- David Geffen (Cofounder, DreamWorks)
- Jerry Weintraub (Hollywood producer)
- Maya Angelou (Poet - Civil Rights Activist)
- David Copperfield (Illusionist)
- Jack Dorsey (Co-founder, Twitter; founder, Square)

## EXECUTIVE

E

Executives do not like to waste time. They are productive and thrive on getting the job done. They are task-oriented and focused on getting results. They do not like small talk. They are good at managing things and people. Executives feel important when they are in control, solving problems, working, providing, and winning. They are happiest when they are pursuing or achieving a desired goal.

### *Strengths*

- Competitive and ambitious
- Have a never-say-die attitude
- Determined to win and are willing to pay the price to do so
- Like a challenge and will not flinch under pressure
- Stable, secure, and give a reassuring sense of being on solid ground
- Hard worker
- Self-starter and focused

### *Weaknesses*

- Can be controlling by promoting their own agenda
- Frustrated when not providing at their desired level
- Cannot tolerate less productive team members and coworkers
- Can feel insecure when they are not winning
- Can be occasionally stubborn and self-centered
- Can be overly competitive and afraid of losing

### *Buying Motives*

Executives are motivated by *Proof*. When purchasing a product or service, they want proof that it works and that it is going to make their life or business better. They respond to third-party testimonials and reviews. Executives focus on the big picture of getting what they want—not the details on how to achieve it.

### *Examples of Successful Executives*

- Phil Knight (Cofounder, Nike)
- Steve Wynn (Casino magnate)
- Ruth Bader Ginsburg (US Supreme Court Justice)
- Enzo Ferrari (Ferrari)
- Michael Phelps (Olympic champion)
- Larry Ellison (Oracle)
- Serena Williams (Tennis Player)
- Floyd "Money" Mayweather (Boxing champion)
- Jay Z (Rapper)
- Harriet Tubman (Abolitionist and political activist)
- John D. Rockefeller (Oil magnate)

## DRIVE Buying Motivation Review

- Director = Lifestyle
- Relator = Community
- Intellectual = Systems
- Validator = Admiration
- Executive = Proof

2

# The Ultimate DRIVE Illustration

"You are so full of sh**! I think there is no chance on God's green earth that this deal could ever possibly close because you would be an idiot among your friends to value this company at $1.5 million or $3 million. It just doesn't add up." *Shark Tank* billionaire Mark Cuban berated Kent Frankovich, who was pitching his bike safety product, Revolights.

In business and on the *Shark Tank*, not every deal goes as planned. But sometimes the stars align, and it goes perfectly. Have you ever watched *Shark Tank*, and the second you saw the pitch, you knew the right shark to make the product successful? Have you seen participants focus on a particular shark because they knew that shark would be a perfect fit? That is the purpose of DRIVE: matching the

right product or service to the right customer to create a win-win scenario.

If you watch closely, you probably noticed that each shark treats investors and potential investments quite differently. Some are aggressive, while others are laid back. Some ask for hard numbers, while others want to hear about their distribution and manufacturing.

All of those differences are because each of the sharks has a different DRIVE. Shark Tank is the perfect real-world illustration of the five components of DRIVE. So, let's analyze five of the top sharks and see how their DRIVE is revealed in the show.

- Director—Robert Herjavec
- Relator—Lori Greiner
- Intellectual—Daymond John
- Validator—Mark Cuban
- Executive—Kevin O'Leary

Fair warning, though: once you read this next section, it may ruin *Shark Tank* for you. You won't be able to un-see each shark and how they perfectly align with their DRIVE. But on the positive side, the more you learn about how to observe others' DRIVE, the more influence and connection you will have with people.

## (D) Robert Herjavec, Director

Kathy Hutchins / Shutterstock.com

Robert Herjavec is spontaneous and adventurous. He is usually the first one who will jump up and try a new product. The products he invests in often fall in the category of lifestyle, from kayaks and custom clothes to cars.

He doesn't invest solely for ROI; he is passionate about products that help others experience life, feel free, be independent, and have a purpose. In short, what makes Robert feel important is his *Lifestyle*—which makes him a clear Director.

Entrepreneur Jason Woods was on Season 3 with his prototype of an electric jet-propelled bodyboard, called Kymera. The sharks were unimpressed. Mark Cuban (Validator) told Woods, "You're not an entrepreneur; you're a want-trepreneur. In ten years, you could not figure out how to make a product and sell it." Daymond John (Intellectual) quickly chimed in: "This is the worst pitch I have ever seen. I am out."

Seven years later, in Season 10, Woods had a shot at redemption. This time, he had a finished product and some sales under his belt: $900,000 in unfulfilled orders due to insufficient capital for manufacturing. He was seeking $250,000 for five percent of his company.

Kevin O'Leary (Executive), seeing the sales and backorders, could smell blood in the water. He pounced with an offer of $250,000 for five percent + $500 royalty per bodyboard, up to $750,000. Daymond John (Intellectual) quickly offered $250,000 for ten percent, sweetening the deal by offering his expertise in manufacturing, distribution, and licensing. Mark Cuban (Validator) and Lori Greiner (Relator) both passed.

Then Robert Herjavec (Director) said enthusiastically, "I love the product. I love this kind of cool, funky, go fast stuff . . . love the second chances. That is what makes this country great: everyone deserves a second chance. I know this space; I think you need more money. I will give you $500,000 for ten percent."

Without hesitation, Woods ignored the other two offers and signed on with Robert. As he and his project manager Adam Majewski were walking out of the tank, Majewski commented, "That was the right partner. That was exactly who we wanted."

Woods is clearly also a Director. He spent seventeen years transforming a prototype into a finished product. He quit his job and raised over half a million dollars to keep his dream alive. Directors are driven by passion—and their passion is to live their life their way. Subconsciously, Woods wanted Herjavec because he felt a kinship with him.

Ironically, Robert overpaid. He could have offered the exact same thing as Daymond—$250,000 for ten percent—and Woods likely would have taken it. That's all because Woods (Director) wants to work with someone like himself. Instead, being a passionate Director, Robert doubled Daymond's offer because he wanted to be in that space.

If you are a Director, do you love activities or experiences that make you feel free and independent? Do you find yourself being spontaneous when you want something? Directors thrive by taking any situation and customizing it to meet their needs. Their superpower is collaborating with different people to create something of greater value. They are visionaries, dreamers, and achievers.

## (R) Lori Greiner, Relator

Kathy Hutchins / Shutterstock.com

Lori Greiner is all about the individual. She faithfully advocates for the little guy, helping the budding entrepreneur get their product onto QVC or on the shelves of Bed Bath & Beyond. You've often seen her invest more in the individual than in the product itself. Her top investments have been in community-based products such as a kid's clothing line, personal care products, and all-natural cleaning products. Lori Greiner is clearly motivated by *Community* and is a Relator.

On Season 4, Ginelle Mills introduced herself as the inventor of Cool Wazoo, a five-in-one baby product that transforms from a changing mat into a shopping cart seat protector. She asked the Sharks for $65,000 in exchange for twenty-five percent equity in her business. She had little traction: $20,000 in revenue in twelve months.

One by one, each shark bowed out. As Lori turned her down, she gave supportive advice, and in the end, Mills broke down in tears. "I have worked so hard," she shared. "I am up at 4 a.m., working entrepreneur hours. I underestimated the time it would take. I did not know it was going to be this hard. I have been working on this for four years. It took me two years to design it and source the materials."

Lori interrupted her then and said, "Ginelle, I am going to come back in. I really like you and I really believe in you. I can see you are going to put your heart and soul into this. I will give you the $65,000 for twenty-five percent." Kevin (the Executive) said, "Wow! I would have asked for fifty percent." But, as a Relator, Lori cared more about the individual than the product. She did not greedily gouge Mills for fifty percent ownership. She did not say she loved the product or was excited to be in the baby diaper mat business. Lori invested because she supports her community of entrepreneurs.

If you are a Relator, have you made a decision based on someone else's interest more than your own? Do you find yourself giving more than you receive? Relators excel at making other people feel important and comfortable. Their superpower is in supporting the team, lifting and inspiring others, and giving back.

## Daymond John, Intellectual

Leonard Zhukovsky / Shutterstock.com

One shark is always the first to ask, "Is it patented?" and, "Where are you having it manufactured?" and demand, "Tell me about your distribution system." That shark is Daymond John. You will notice when he tries to attract a potential partner, he offers his manufacturing, distribution, and shipping systems. His top investments are all manufacturing-related, from motorcycle helmets to patented insoles to racing drones. Daymond John is motivated by *Systems* and is an Intellectual.

In Season 6, Patrick Whaley sought an investment in TITIN, his line of weighted compression gear, asking $500,000 for five percent of his company. Whaley was struggling with inventory management and manufacturing. The final two offers came in from Kevin O'Leary, at $500,000 for fifteen percent, and Daymond John, at $500,000 for twenty percent.

Even though Daymond was asking for five percent more than Kevin, Whaley took Daymond's offer. He saw Daymond's Intellectual specialization in creating logistical solutions to manufacturing and distribution challenges.

When selling your product or services, price is not always the best competitive advantage. What matters most is how your product or service pairs with the needs of another's DRIVE, as in Patrick Whaley's case with TITIN.

If you are an Intellectual—be honest—do you sometimes feel like you are the smartest person in the room? Do you find it hard or frustrating when you share information or a solution with someone and they don't implement it? Intellectuals thrive on organizing and systemizing as well as learning new information. Their superpower is seeing a challenge and being able to find a solution.

## (V) Mark Cuban, Validator

Jaguar PS / Shutterstock.com

Mark Cuban is a Validator. He is motivated by *Admiration*. Validators have a superpower to motivate and inspire others. Many times, you will see Mark give support and encouragement to an underdog by inspiring them to follow their dreams, even when they don't find a deal in the tank. Validators are the ultimate cheerleaders.

Conversely, when a Validator feels offended or violated, they can quickly become critical. At times, when Mark feels threatened by another shark, he will verbally challenge them, as he did with guest shark Chris Sacca (angel investor in Twitter, Uber, Instagram, and Kickstarter) on Season 7.

Here's the story: Dave Vasen, founder of Brightwheel, was seeking $400,000 for four percent of his childcare management app. Two sharks were in for the agreed price, and Mark wanted in with Chris.

When Chris did not want Mark as a partner, Mark berated Chris, saying, "When he assigns his name to it, it holds a lot of street cred in his little part of the world. But once you get out of that little bubble called Silicon Valley, it doesn't mean sh**!" The jabs went back and forth for a bit, but Mark did eventually partner with Chris and invest in Brightwheel.

If you are a Validator, do you find you have a short fuse when people disrespect you? Do you find yourself getting defensive in business or in negotiations? Once again, a Validator's superpower is in validating others. They have the ability to encourage people to perform at a higher level. Many top Validators have overcome unbeatable odds. Mark Cuban used to sleep on a friend's couch with less than twenty dollars to his name; now his net worth is more than $4 billion.

## Kevin O'Leary, Executive

Kathy Hutchins / Shutterstock.com

Kevin O'Leary (Mr. Wonderful) is an Executive who is motivated by *Proof*. His mantra is simple: "Show me the money." He is the first to ask, "What are your sales numbers?" When he no longer likes what he is hearing, he will say something like, "You are dead to me!" or, "I am not trying to make friends—you want a friend, buy a dog. I am trying to make money." His top investments are in the lucrative wedding and alcohol and spirits industries.

On Season 4, brothers Yuen and Peter Young were trying to raise $1 million for twelve percent of their sushi company. All four sharks were out, but Kevin saw the potential of How Do You Roll and offered $1 million for twenty-two percent. The other sharks gasped and tried to convince these two brothers to not take the deal, but Kevin batted them down, finally settling on $1 million for twenty percent.

As the two sushi company owners turned to walk out of the tank, Barbara told them, "You made a deal with the devil." Kevin isn't the devil. He knows what he wants, knows his numbers, and has an iron will to go after it. That is the heart of an Executive: to have control and to win.

If you are an Executive, do you find you like control and want to win? Are you driven to reach your goals and provide security? Executives' superpower is their ability to focus on a desired outcome and stick with it until it is accomplished. They are driven to succeed, and they will do whatever it takes to make it happen.

What is your Superpower? Every DRIVE has a superpower that allows you to overcome unbeatable odds, to rise above incredible challenges, and to charge forward when most people retreat. Next, we'll explore how to tap into your superpower.

# 3

# The DRIVE Superpower

How did a high school dropout become a billionaire and owner of some of the most coveted brands? How did a bankrupt used-tire salesman build the largest tire retailer in the world? How did an average college student become the founder of the first American company to have a billion dollars in revenue? How did a no-name twenty-five-year-old become one of the biggest Hollywood producers of our time? How did a boxer become the highest-paid athlete in history?

It all comes down to their DRIVE and how they tapped into their unique superpowers. In this chapter, you'll discover your own superpower and how you can use it to succeed. For now, just read the DRIVE that pertains to you. When you want to market or sell to the other four DRIVEs, come back and study theirs.


- Director pg. 31
- Relator pg. 43
- Intellectual pg. 53
- Validator pg. 61
- Executive pg. 69

## Director

D

"You will either end up incarcerated or a millionaire!" exclaimed the headmaster of Richard Branson's high school as he was dropping out.

Both predictions came true. After leaving school at age sixteen, Branson started his own magazine about music and youth culture, called *The Student*. As the editor-in-chief of the magazine, he began advertising the sale of records in the publication. His small record business was an overnight success. Because everyone involved in his company had virtually no experience in life or business, he decided to call it "Virgin."

Like other Directors, Richard Branson was (and is) motivated and influenced by creating his ideal lifestyle. He achieved that through three core channels:

- Being **free and independent** and **experiencing life** on his terms
- **Overcoming obstacles** and working toward his **life's purpose**
- Being **creative**, maintaining his **appearance**, and **performing**

A Director's confidence stems from feeling free and independent. This sense of freedom makes them feel successful.

Years after dropping out of high school, Branson impulsively wanted to take his girlfriend, Joan, on a trip to the Virgin Islands. He'd heard rumors that if you expressed real interest in buying an island, they would fly you around in a private helicopter and put you up in a grand villa.

He made a few calls to some local agents. As he embellished the size of his record business, the artists he had signed, and the expansion of his company to the islands where he could bring his rock stars for a get-away, the real estate agents began to get very excited.

Richard and Joan spent two pampered days visiting islands and staying in sumptuous villas. They saw three different locations and pretended to be interested in purchasing two. He asked if there were any more.

"There's one more, which is a real little jewel," the agent said. "It's being sold by a British lord who's never even been here. It's called Necker Island, but I don't think it's a wise idea because it's miles from anywhere." This made Branson want to see it even more.

As they toured the island, it was everything he never knew he wanted. He and Joan hiked to the highest hill, where he could see the coral reef that surrounded most of the island. The water was so clear he could see stingrays swimming and where the leatherback turtles came ashore to lay their eggs.

"How much does he want for it?" Branson asked.

"£3 million."

"Nice thought," said Joan as they trudged back to the helicopter.

"How much were you thinking of spending?" the agent asked, suddenly smelling a rat.

"We could offer £150,000," Richard said brightly. Then, "$200,000," trying to make it sound like more.

"I see," replied the agent.

As they arrived back at their villa, it was obvious they were no longer welcome. Their bags were packed and waiting outside the door. They were basically kicked off the island, as if they were some type of cattle rustlers or carpetbaggers. But as a Director, this only made Richard more determined to return and buy Necker Island.

Directors live in a world where anything and everything is possible. Some people might say they are not in touch with reality, but as you read the different stories of Directors, you will see they simply create their own reality. They do not play by the rules—but not because they don't believe in rules and structure. They just don't think others' rules apply to them.

On the way home, Richard and Joan tried to catch a flight to Puerto Rico. However, the scheduled flight was canceled. The airport was full of stranded passengers. Richard quickly contacted a few charter companies, wrangling a deal to charter an entire plane to Puerto Rico. He calculated the cost of the plane and divided it by the number of seats it had.

Then he borrowed a blackboard and wrote, "Virgin Airways—$39 one-way trip to Puerto Rico." He walked up and down the terminal with his blackboard until every seat was sold—and Virgin Airlines was born.

Back in London, he used some creative due diligence to find out more about Necker Island's English Lord. He discovered that the owner was actually in a hurry to sell to be able to construct a building in Scotland. The building was going to cost him £200,000.

Richard quickly raised his offer to buy the island to £175,000 and waited three months. Finally, he got a call: "If you offer £180,000, it's yours."

There was one stipulation, though. The government declared that whoever bought Necker Island would have to develop it within five years or ownership would revert to the government.

Branson had two options: not buy Necker Island, or make more money to be able to afford the development. Directors love a good challenge. Obstacles are only part of the game for them. He jumped in headfirst and bought Necker Island.

Whether he was buying a fifteen-room manor at age twenty-one with no money to his name, buying an island at a fraction of the asking price, or creating an airline company just to get a ride home, Richard Branson emulates the soul of a Director. He's spontaneous, driven to be free, and independent, with a desire to experience life to the fullest.

You can confirm this by scanning the titles of Branson's books:

- *Screw It, Let's Do it*
- *The Virgin Way—If It's Not Fun, It's Not Worth Doing*
- *Losing My Virginity—How I Survived, Had Fun, and Made a Fortune Doing Business My Way*

If you are a Director, does Branson's life appeal to you? Do you want to travel the world and experience life on your terms? Do you see the possible in the impossible?

Directors are in pursuit of their own mission. They get laser-focused on what they want to achieve and often ignore the details or consequences. This is their superpower and their kryptonite.

### *Superpower vs. Kryptonite (Strengths vs. Weaknesses)*

A Director's superpower is their ability to be committed to their life's purpose and to inspire others to do the same. They are often entrepreneurially minded and believe they can do anything. They feel free and independent, and approach the world through their creativity and ability to perform under pressure. This is most evident when you look at Elon Musk and the challenges he has faced building three different billion-dollar companies.

Over the last twenty years, Elon Musk has been the brains behind some of the world's most innovative technological endeavors, including PayPal, Tesla Motors, and the rocket ship company SpaceX. His latest high-speed transportation idea, dubbed "the Hyperloop," sounds like a completely unrealistic science fiction fantasy. But considering his life accomplishments thus far, nothing seems to be impossible for him. As you look at his challenges, ask yourself, "At what point would I have given up?"

On the road to becoming Elon Musk:

- 1995—Turned down for a job at Netscape
- 1996—Fired as CEO of his own company, Zip2
- 1999—First PayPal product was voted as one of the ten worst business ideas
- 1999—Crashed his newly purchased $1 million McLaren F1
- 2000—Personally funded PayPal and saved it from bankruptcy, only to be ousted while on his honeymoon
- 2000—Nearly died from cerebral malaria while on vacation
- 2001—Russians refused to sell him rockets to experiment with space travel
- 2002—Russians reject him again after raising the price to $21 million a rocket
- 2002—Creates SpaceX to build his own rockets
- 2003—Cofounds Tesla Motors
- 2006—First launch with SpaceX—rocket explodes
- 2007—Second launch—second explosion
- 2008—Third launch—third explosion (critical failure as it was transporting a NASA satellite)
- 2008—The world's most viewed auto program, *Top Gear*, reviews the Tesla Roadster and dubs it a "barely running experiment"
- 2008—Both Tesla and SpaceX are on the verge of bankruptcy
- 2008—Gets divorced
- 2013—First rocket failure during experimental drone ship landing
- 2014—Model S has three public battery fires
- 2015—Fourth rocket explosion at launch, and second and third explosions during experimental drone ship landings

- 2016—Model X deliveries delayed more than eighteen months
- 2016—Fifth rocket explosion during a test with Facebook's AMOS-6 satellite (worth $300 million)
- 2016—Fourth, fifth, and sixth failures during experimental drone ship landings
- 2017—Merlin rocket explodes on testing
- 2017—Long-term delays in the production of Tesla's Model 3
- 2018—Tesla voluntarily recalls 123,000 Model S vehicles for issues with the power steering components
- 2018—Tesla posts its largest quarterly loss

A Director's strength lies in their inexorable desire to create the life they want, no matter the cost. This does not mean all Directors want to be billionaires like Branson and Musk. They are motivated to create the lifestyle they want, even if it is a simple lifestyle. They are driven and spontaneous, and often do not pay attention to the rules in their quest for happiness.

When not kept in check, though, their superpower can also be their kryptonite. Their weakness stems from being too impulsive and spontaneous, and not properly weighing the consequences of their decisions.

Between 500,000–700,000 motorcyclists descend on the Black Hills of South Dakota every August for the annual Sturgis Rally. Being a red-blooded American and a Director, I have always been fascinated with the rally. While at a seminar, the CEO of a $25 million company and his top lieutenant invited me to go.

When the time came, we trailered our bikes and traveled the 642 miles to Sturgis. The Black Hills were gorgeous, with winding roads and evergreen trees. The views were breathtaking. On the second day, we rode from our hotel in Rapid City through the back roads to Sturgis. With four type-A personalities, we continued to pick up speed around each curve. Coming around one bend, I watched one of

our friends, Willey, lay his bike down just too far—and slide directly off the cliff.

I pulled my bike over and immediately followed the skid marks on the concrete to where the bike took a chunk out of a tree before it descended at full speed, tumbling end over end. I shimmied down the

hillside, holding on to the roots of trees for stability. Being the first responder, I feared the worst. I expected to find him dead.

Fortunately, some trees had slowed his fall, and he did not drop to the river below. The bike was totaled, and he was rushed to the

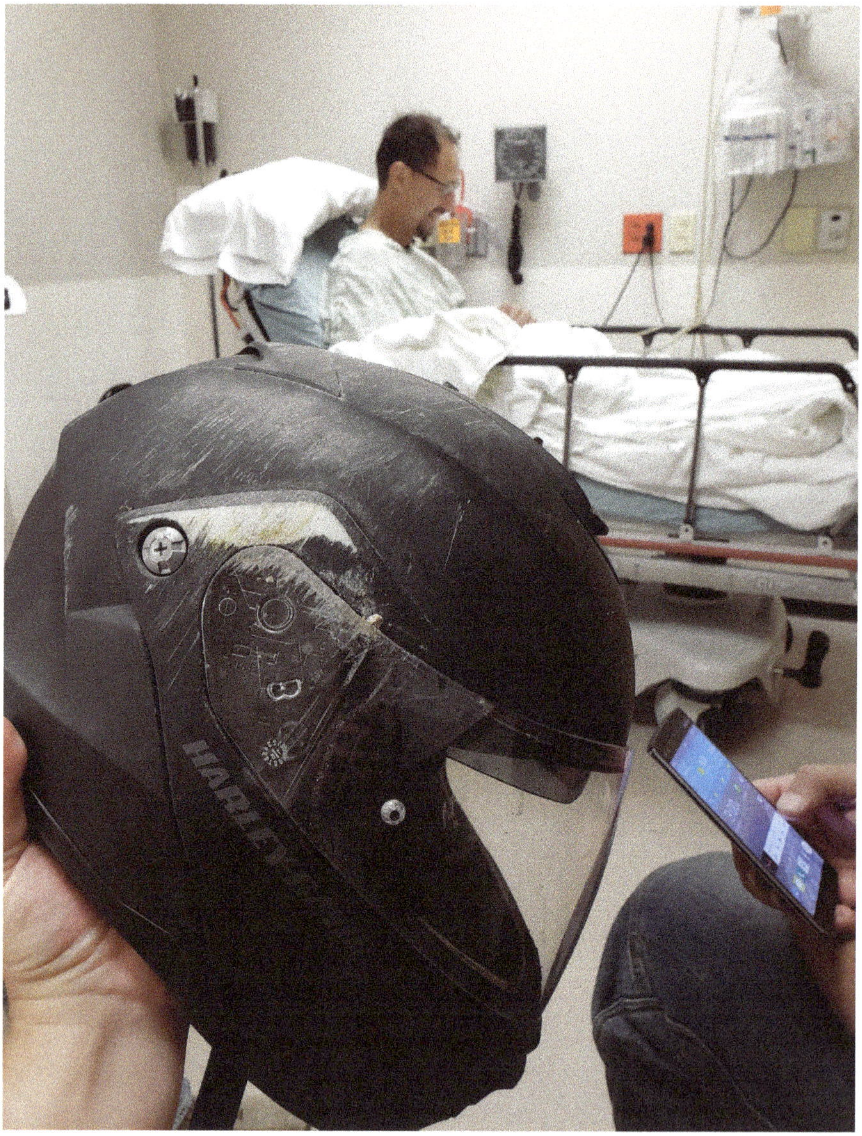

hospital. After a few broken ribs and a shattered collarbone had been tended to, he was stitched up and taken back to the hotel to rest.

The next morning at breakfast, I came clean. I had never ridden a motorcycle before. I'd never ridden over twenty-five miles per hour, in the rain, or at night; I didn't have a motorcycle license; and I had only bought my motorcycle six days earlier. As the group picked their jaws up off the table, I realized the impulsive nature of a Director. They don't tend to focus on the details. Staying focused in general is difficult. They tend to be big-picture thinkers.

Here's another example. It was a balmy, humid Cancun day. I had just walked off stage from my presentation and taken my seat at the VIP table at the back of the Hard Rock Convention Center. My client, seven-time Mr. Olympian, seven-time Mr. World, and seven-time Mr. Universe for natural bodybuilding, Ron Williams, was next on stage.

We had traveled and spoken together many times. I had personally seen the physical transformations he had assisted my other clients with. He is by far one of the best at what he does. As he was presenting his weight-loss program, showing his before-and-after transformations, one of the top income earners of the company, Scott Rowe, leaned over and said, "I will bet my motorcycle against your motorcycle that I can lose more weight than you."

What I should have said was, "No, I am going to hire Ron!" Instead, I immediately said, "*Absolutely!*" Four months later, after losing, I transferred my bike title to him.

The weakness of a Director is their impulsive nature to make irrational decisions based on something that would be fun. They are driven by *Lifestyle*, which causes them to not analyze the pros and cons of each decision.

## D *How to Sell to a Director*

Each DRIVE has seven associated keywords. On social media or in your advertisements, you can target specific DRIVEs when you use those keywords. In future chapters, we will go into greater detail for each keyword. But for now, here is a quick snapshot. When selling to a Director, make sure the benefits of your product or service helps them to:

- Be **free** and **independent**
- **Experience life** at a whole new level
- Assist them in **overcoming** obstacles
- Work toward their **life's purpose**
- Be more **creative**
- Enhance their **appearance**
- **Perform** at a higher level

## Relator

R

Is losing $15 million in potential revenue every year worth supporting your community? Discount Tire repairs over 1,560,000 tires every year for free—whether you bought your tires from them or not. According to Bruce Halle, the founder of Discount Tires, "By repairing customers' tires at no charge, they are very grateful, and we've made a customer for life."

Like all Relators, Bruce is motivated and influenced by *Community*. He achieves it through three core channels:

- **Influence, relationships, family, friends**, and **parenting**
- **Giving, serving**, and **volunteering**
- **Spirituality** (as defined by them)

Relators' confidence stems from the health of their relationships. If they feel they are in a caring trusted relationship, they feel successful.

Bruce started as a failure. Three years after borrowing money from a friend to buy a minority share of a tire company, it went under. All it left him was six tires, a few gas caps, and considerable debt.

While trying to pay off his debts, he realized he needed to sell just six tires a day: five to cover the bills and debt payments, and one to turn a profit to feed his family. For years, he and one employee worked tirelessly in his store in Ann Arbor, Michigan.

As success slowly came, he opened the next store. And the next. And the next. Halle's qualities of being a Relator—community and service—have permeated the culture of Discount Tires for nearly sixty years. Their slogan is "America's Neighborhood Tire Store."

DISCOUNT® TIRE

Discount Tires is now 1,000 stores strong, with over 10,000 employees and $4.5 billion in annual sales. They have become the largest privately owned tire retailer in the world. Bruce is the richest person in Arizona, with a net worth of $5.5 billion.

As a Relator, he believed in promoting from within, which is why nearly all of the firm's 10,000 employees (with the exception of some in the legal, financial, and information technology departments) started out changing tires in the company's stores. This includes most of the company's top executives.

Relators make personal and business decisions based on how they will impact other people. In an interview with TireBusiness.com, Bruce explained why he promotes from within:

> I will not go out and hire some MBA graduate from whatever college. . . . If I were to bring somebody in at a higher level without having worked in the stores, I may as well get in my car, drive around to 1,000 stores, and slap every one of my guys in the face—that's literally what I've done to them. And I would never do that, and neither would any of my people.

This philosophy helps explain why Discount Tire has little employee turnover. Citing members of the company's executive staff, Mr. Halle noted many have been with the company for more than thirty or forty years. "I could count them on two hands, in all these years, the people that have left," he said.

A major focus for Relators is giving back to their communities. "I might be living here in Arizona, but we have over 100 stores in Texas," Halle said. "That's our community, too. And so is Colorado and Michigan, and all the different states around. Those are our communities; our people live there. It's our responsibility to support that community and their needs the best we can."

I brought my own car into Discount Tire one day with a flat tire. As they were taking off the custom rims, they scratched one. Without flinching, they said they would have my rims painted and repaired by a professional detailer or give me the tire for free. The tire was $527.

I was shocked at a company that would empower their employees to take care of their customers without hesitation. Then I found a quote by Discount Tires Vice Chairman Gary Van Brunt: "You have to have integrity in everything you do. If something isn't right, make it right. Fix it. Don't cut corners. Make it right, because people are relying on us." Not only did they make it right for me, but they also now have a customer for life.

### *Superpower vs. Kryptonite (Strengths vs. Weaknesses)*

Relators are motivated to take care of the *Community.* They are phenomenal networkers who connect family and friends together to solve larger problems. They are service-minded and constantly think of how they can give back. Whether it serves them or not, Relators care about other people before thinking about themselves. This is both their superpower and their kryptonite.

Consider TOMS Shoes, a company that gives away a pair of shoes for every pair you buy. On a trip to Argentina, founder Blake Mycoskie ran into an American woman in a café who was doing a shoe fundraiser. Intrigued, he followed her from village to village to see for himself the pain and suffering of poverty-stricken children who were without shoes.

After leaving, he continued to research how big this problem really was. He knew nothing about manufacturing shoes or the shoe

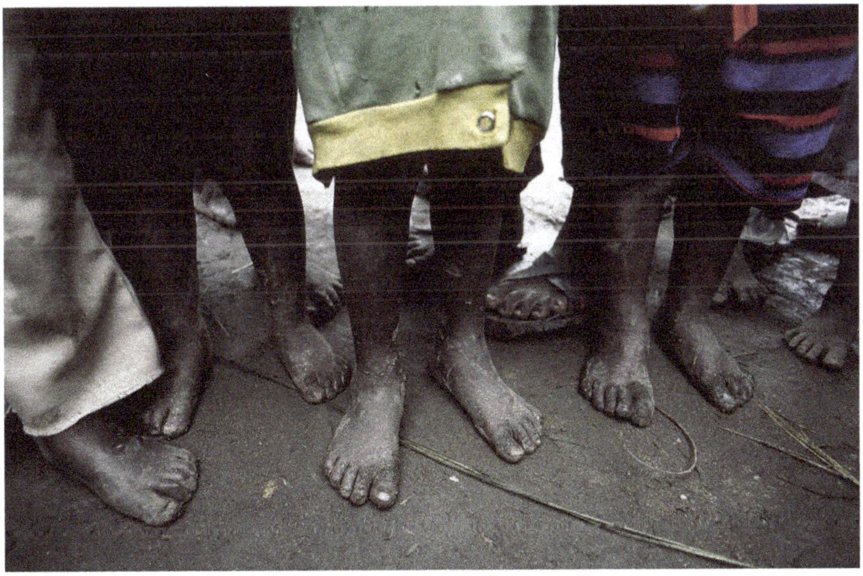

industry; but as a Relator, he knew he would never forgive himself if he did not try to help. So, he did what any Relator would do: he reached out to his network to see who could help him.

Through his relationships, he found a manufacturer and retailers willing to carry his shoes. Since its founding in 2006, TOMS Shoes has given away more than eighty-six million pairs to children in need.

The TOMS "One for One" model has also inspired many other companies to adopt a similar concept. Warby Parker, launched in 2010, donates a pair of glasses to someone in need for every pair of glasses it sells. One World Play has donated over a million indestructible soccer balls to schools in third-world countries. Soapbox, which sells personal hygiene products, has also donated over a million units to those in need.

Relators excel in impacting social injustices and culture. Think Mother Teresa and Gandhi—both Relators. A modern hero of social injustice was Fred Rogers, better known as Mister Rogers from Mister Rogers' Neighborhood. This seemingly insignificant public television show from the 1960s has had a lasting impact on generations.

The '60s brought with it the turmoil of the civil rights era. Under the Jim Crow–era policy, blacks and whites could not swim at the same time—and many pools were entirely off-limits to blacks. In a horrific image from 1964, a hotel manager is seen dumping acid into a pool of swimmers, both black and white, while a startled and fearful black woman clings to a white man, screaming in terror.

Within four months after Dr. Martin Luther King, Jr. was shot and killed, Mister Rogers hired Francois Clemmons, the first African American to have a recurring role on a children's television program. On Episode 1065, the show opens with Mister Rogers filling a plastic pool in his front yard as Clemens, the singing policeman, approaches. Mister Rogers invites him to share the pool with him.

Clemmons quickly accepts, rolls up the pant legs of his uniform, and places his very brown feet in the same water as Rogers' very white feet. This seems insignificant now, but then it was quite controversial. Rogers did not care; he believed everyone was welcome in his neighborhood.

Relators are courageous and fearless when it comes to helping and protecting their community. They will go to almost any length to help those in need—even to their own detriment.

On May 1, 1969, Fred Rogers testified before the Senate Committee on Communications to speak out against $20 million in funding being stripped from public television. His nemesis was a brash, hardheaded

senator and subcommittee chairman, Senator John Pastore. During the two days of hearings and testimonies, Senator Pastore would hold a stopwatch and cut off anyone who was over their time.

He knew nothing of Rogers or his show. At first, the Senator was very caustic toward him. Rogers told him how he used to do the show on a thirty dollar budget, making all the puppets and sets as well as writing the scripts and songs. Pastore was surprised and began to soften a little toward him. Mr. Rogers continued to express his concerns for children who are only exposed to cartoons where they see characters being hit with oversized sledgehammers and having gunfights. Pastore expressed that he shared the same concern.

Mr. Rogers said, "And this is what I give. I give an expression of care, every day, to each child. To help him realize that he is unique. I end the program by saying, 'You've made this day a special day by just your being you. There's no person in the whole world like you. And I like you just the way you are.'"

With only six minutes to make his case for public television, and having already used five minutes, Mr. Rogers asked if he could share a song he had written for children. He boldly began to sing:

> What do you do with the mad that you feel when you feel so mad you could bite?
> When the whole wide world seems oh-so-wrong, and nothing you do seems very right?
> What do you do? Do you punch a bag? Do you pound some clay or some dough?
> Do you round up friends for a game of tag or see how fast you go?
> It's great to be able to stop when you've planned a thing that's wrong.
> And be able to do something else instead and think this song. I can stop when I want to, can stop when I wish, can stop, stop, stop, anytime.
> And what a good feeling to feel like this. And know that the feeling is really mine.
> Know that there's something deep inside that helps us become what we can.
> For a girl can be someday a lady, and a boy can be someday a man.

With a stunned, shocked look on his face, Senator Pastore said, "I think it's wonderful. I think it's wonderful. It looks like you just earned the $20 million."

The gentleness and kindness a Relator uses to convey their message has the ability to soften the hardest heart. At times, this kindness can also be their kryptonite, letting them be taken advantage of. Relators find it hard to stand up for themselves when dealing with others. They care so much for their community that they will sacrifice their own best interest to not offend or hurt someone else.

The example I'm about to share is extreme—but when I heard it, I was so shocked and knew it had to be written. Claire wanted to surprise her boyfriend by cleaning his room and making dinner for them. As she put away his laundry, she found an engagement ring in his top dresser drawer, hidden under the socks.

Her heart pounded in her chest. They had only been dating for four months, and she had felt a bond with him, but she wasn't sure he felt the same way. Now she had proof! He loved her, and he was ready to commit to a lasting marriage.

With all the excitement, she wanted to convey her love for him, so she finished cleaning the house, went to the store, and bought bridal magazines, flowers, and made a large helium balloon sign that said "YES!" After decorating his apartment with all the enthusiasm of a bride-to-be, she waited on pins and needles for him to walk in.

He walked in and saw rose petals on the floor, bridal pictures cut out from magazines decorating the walls, and the large inflated "YES!" At first, he was confused, not knowing what she was implying. Then he saw it.

The wedding ring his ex-fiancée had given back to him when she called off the wedding. Being a Relator and not wanting to disappoint his over-the-moon girlfriend, he went along with the "proposal." They were married for just under three years.

This is a true story. The boyfriend is my assistant's brother. Being a Relator, his kryptonite was not being able to stand up for himself in his relationships. While this is not the case for all Relators, if you are a Relator or know someone who is, you likely have similar stories about sacrificing on behalf of someone else.

A Relator's superpower is to think more of the group than of themselves. In weakness, though, they tend to not stand up for what they want and will not make their desires known so as not to offend the group.

## R *How to Sell to a Relator*

Each DRIVE has seven associated keywords. On social media or in your advertisements, you can target specific DRIVEs when you use those keywords. In future chapters, we will go into greater detail for each keyword. But for now, here is a quick snapshot. When selling to a Relator, make sure the benefits of your product or service helps them to:

- Have a power of **influence**
- Enhance their **relationships**
- Strengthen their **family**
- Be better **parents** (providing for their kids emotionally, physically, and financially)
- Deepen their relationships with their **friends**
- Provide **service** to others
- Connect to **God, Spirit, or Universe** (spirituality as defined by them)

WELCOME
TO Fabulous
LAS VEGAS
NEVADA

## Intellectual

I

His palms were sweaty as he sat down at the blackjack table in the smoke-filled casino. Only two years earlier, he was flush with $92 million in investment money. Now, with only $5,000 to his name, he did not have enough for payroll.

It was Friday night in Las Vegas, and Fred Smith was stuck between a rock and a hard place. He would have to earn a 625 percent return on his money in the next forty-eight hours, or he would lose everything—including his fledging business, Federal Express.

Before FedEx, both the U.S. Postal Service and UPS had worked on the challenge of making overnight deliveries a reality using established systems and theories. They thought logically in terms of packages and points of location. For example, if you want to connect one hundred markets with one another, and if you do it all with direct point-to-point deliveries, it will take 100 × 99, or 9,900 direct deliveries. They concluded that there was no way they could make it economically feasible.

But Fred Smith was an Intellectual, and was thus motivated and influenced by *Systems*. For intellectuals, that is achieved through three core channels:

- They seek **knowledge** and **learning**
- They have high **standards** and are well **organized**
- They cherish being in the **moment** and in **nature**, as well as being **health** conscious

Their confidence stems from what they know and whether they can use a system to be successful.

So, Fred Smith did not think in terms of delivering packages within established systems. While attending Yale University in the mid-1960s, Smith wrote an economics term paper on the need for reliable overnight delivery in the Information Age.

As an Intellectual, he wondered about the concept of movement and thought about how things are moved from one place to another. He thought about how information is moved and how banks move money around the world. Both information systems and banks, he discovered, put all points in a network, and connect them through a central hub. His professor was unimpressed with his term paper and responded, "The concept is interesting and well-formed, but in order to earn better than a C, the idea must be feasible."

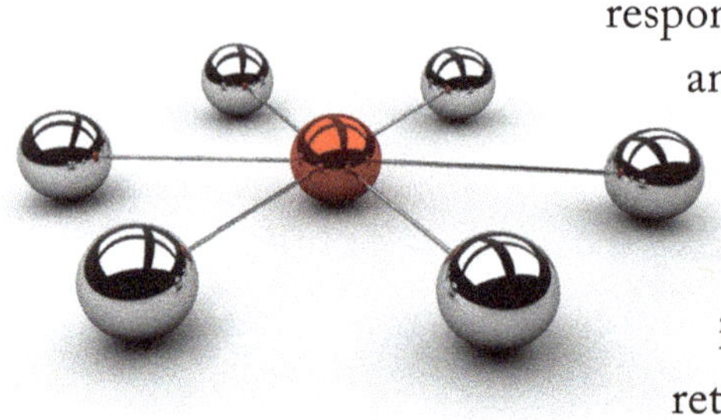

After graduation and serving in the Vietnam War, Fred returned to his idea of creating an overnight delivery system. He formed Federal Express (now FedEx) in 1971. He raised $90 million from investors and venture capitalists. On opening night, he had fourteen Falcon jets and a fleet of vans connecting twenty-two cities.

The new company spent heavily on advertising with the slogan "FedEx—When it absolutely, positively has to be there overnight." The first night of operation was inauspicious, with only 186 packages shipped.

Being an Intellectual, Smith continued to create systems that would make FedEx the $60-billion behemoth it is today. He created the first real-time tracking of packages and brought robots and autonomous vehicles into the warehouses so humans could focus on high-value objectives. He saved 177 million gallons of jet fuel by upgrading his planes and revamping their shipping routes.

But it wasn't always a success. Back to the smoke-filled casino . . .

Two years after Smith founded the company, it was in trouble. The oil embargo of 1973 caused a gas shortage and sent the cost of automotive and aircraft fuel skyrocketing. Federal Express was losing more than $1 million a month and was on the verge of bankruptcy.

Smith tried to get loans and find investors who could contribute capital, but no one was interested.

Federal Express's pilots began using their personal credit cards to buy fuel for the planes and keep their deliveries on schedule. The company hit its lowest point when it had just $5,000 left in its accounts. Smith flew to Virginia and approached General Dynamics with one final plea for more funding. They turned him down. FedEx was dead in the water.

Smith wasn't ready to give up. Instead of taking a flight back home to Memphis, he took his last $5,000 and flew to Las Vegas to take his chances at the blackjack tables. On Monday morning, when FedEx's executives came into the office expecting the worst, they were shocked to find the company had $32,000 in its bank account.

The $27,000 Smith had won at the blackjack tables was just enough money to pay for the fuel to keep their planes flying for a few more days. And as luck would have it, a few more days was all FedEx needed. Smith was able to raise $11 million to keep the company in business.

Two years later, in 1976, the company turned its first profit: $3.6 million. Four years later, profits were almost $40 million, and the company's gross revenue was close to half a billion dollars. It went on to be America's first billion-dollar company.

To fully understand the power of that senior economic term paper, look at FedEx statistics today. Revenue in 2019 was $69 billion. The company delivers fifteen million packages a day, employs 450,000 employees, connects 99 percent of the global GDP, runs 678 aircraft serving 650 airports, and operates 180,000 vehicles with services in 220 countries. As an Intellectual, Smith could essentially see the future of how overnight shipping could change the world with the right system in place.

### *Superpower vs. Kryptonite (Strengths vs. Weaknesses)*

Intellectuals are phenomenal at creating processes and systems that create efficiency and profitability. This is both their superpower and their kryptonite.

Les Wexner was born into a working-class Russian immigrant family. Throughout his youth, he worked in his father's clothing store. As an Intellectual, he had different ideas of how his father should run the business. Wexner wanted to create more efficient processes to increase profitability. He analyzed which products sold quickly and those that stayed in the store too long. This caused a lot of friction between him and his father, and eventually Les was fired.

With his analytics in hand, he acquired a bank loan for $5,000 and opened his first Limited store, which specialized in women's athletic wear. As the company grew, he was a pioneer in using computers to control shipments, inventory, and management.

When competition in the athletic apparel sector increased, he opened a manufacturing plant and hired his own designers; his turnaround time for new designs was suddenly quicker than his competitors, who were waiting for the next year's fashion shows. The Limited grew quickly as he continued to refine its processes.

Wexner was so adept at making systems that he started buying other people's companies. In 1982, Roy Raymond, the founder of Victoria's Secret, began to have problems with his business. Victoria's Secret had five stores and a catalog business that was going into bankruptcy. Wexner picked it up for $1 million. Through Wexner's execution, he was able to turn Victoria's Secret into a 1,000 store success, doing $10 billion in retail sales.

Also in 1982, he acquired 207 Lane Bryant stores. He then bought 798 Lerner stores. Wexner continued to develop and buy companies including Abercrombie & Fitch, Bath & Body Works, Structure,

Express, C. O. Bigelow, The White Barn Candle Company, and New York & Company.

This Russian immigrant became a billionaire and now runs one of the largest retail conglomerates. As an Intellectual, he mastered turning other people's problems into a successful process through established systems.

An Intellectual's superpower is their ability to use their intelligence and create profitable systems. Their kryptonite can be their overthinking, which turns into analysis paralysis. They are so focused on getting the process right that they often don't take any risks. For the fear they might be wrong, they rely more on what they know than on experimenting on the chance of a new discovery.

At the age of forty-three, Milton Hershey was the largest manufacturer of caramels in the United States. That same year, he sold his caramel company for $1 million, with the condition that he would not go back into the caramel business.

With his newfound wealth and free time, Hershey focused on a project he hoped could change the world: he wanted to build a town that would be a model of an ideal society. Knowing a town would need an industry, he decided to build his town around the production of chocolate. In 1902, he scouted the east coast for an ideal location for his Chocolate Town.

He settled on Dauphin County, Pennsylvania, a mile from where he was born. In 1903, construction began on a huge, modern chocolate factory. But after several years and hundreds of failed attempts, he did not have a recipe that worked to make milk chocolate. He spent a small fortune on the best minds, from chemists to collegiate professionals, but no one could crack the code to milk chocolate.

One day, Hershey inspected a vat filled with a silky milk solution that blended easily with the chocolate. The worker who created

the solution, John Schmalback, was not one of Hershey's college-educated chemists; he was a regular floor employee. Schmalback had nothing to lose, so he had experimented with no hesitation.

Schmalback's simple breakthrough had been to dissolve a high concentration of sugar in the milk and then boil it slowly at low temperature in a vacuum. The college-educated Intellectuals Hershey had hired spent years trying methods they thought would work. Paralysis by analysis stopped them from taking a risk.

Intellectuals are very intelligent and like to find the best system to make their life and business more efficient. They get frustrated when others hold them back by not following an established system or set of rules.

## I How to Sell to an Intellectual

Each DRIVE has seven associated keywords. On social media or in your advertisements, you can target specific DRIVEs when you use those keywords. In future chapters, we will go into greater detail for each keyword. But for now, here is a quick snapshot. When selling to an Intellectual, make sure the benefits of your product or service helps them to:

- Increase their **knowledge**
- **Learn** something new
- Honor their **standards**
- Be more **organized**
- Be in the **moment**
- Connect with **nature**
- Increase their **health**

## Validator

Ⓥ

Do I need to be liked?
Absolutely not.
I liked to be liked. I enjoy being liked.
I have to be liked.
But it is not like this compulsive need to be liked, like my need to be praised.
—Michael Scott (Manager, Dunder Mifflin)

With sweat running down his face, Jerry Weintraub woke up from a dream where he saw the marquee at the famous Madison Square Garden: "Jerry Weintraub Presents Elvis Presley." It was a motivating dream for the twenty-five-year-old.

What could be more powerful for a Validator than to have his name next to Elvis Presley? He immediately called Elvis's longtime manager, Tom Parker—known as "the Colonel": "My name is Jerry Weintraub, and I want to take Elvis on the road."

"Elvis does not perform live anymore. He's doing movies." The Colonel continued, "Since I have never heard of you, I assume you are a nobody, and therefore I am not interested." Then he hung up. It crushed Jerry to be so harshly reminded that he was a twenty-five-year-old nobody.

Validators are motivated and influenced by *Admiration*. They achieve this through three core channels:

- **Trust** and **respect**
- Giving and receiving **praise, recognition**, and **validation**
- Being **needed** and **acceptance**

Validators are the greatest supporters. They will cheer you along to the end. One of their superpowers is confidence when they trust, accept, and praise themselves.

Even though he had no expertise as an event promoter, Weintraub trusted in himself. With nowhere else to start, he called the Colonel every day. Weeks, months, and then a year went by. Finally, the Colonel asked one day, "You still want to take my boy on the road?"

"Yes, sir," replied Weintraub.

"Then bring me a check for $1 million to the roulette table at the Hilton Hotel in Las Vegas by 9 a.m. tomorrow."

A million dollars was a lot of money in the sixties. That was Rockefeller money. Jerry certainly did not have that kind of money. Being a Validator, he would have to trust and believe in himself to do the impossible. To pull off the task, he created a phone tree to call everyone he knew to help him raise the money.

Through one of his relationships, he found a successful radio station owner from Seattle, who was a huge Elvis fan. Like any good businessman, he wanted a prospectus, a business plan, and a contract.

Jerry said, "I agree with you, but we have *hours* to make this happen. Wire the money to Vegas, and I will pick it up there and get you a contract later." (Imagine asking a complete stranger to wire you a million dollars to Las Vegas!)

The radio owner asked, "What do I get?" Weintraub said, "I will give you half of my business promoting Elvis." Shockingly, the man obliged and wired the money to Vegas.

Due to the lack of available flights from the east coast, it was impossible to make it to Las Vegas by 9 a.m. Weintraub asked the Colonel for a twenty-four-hour extension, which was promptly declined. He was, however, able to secure an extension to 3 p.m.

Just before 3 p.m., Jerry found the Colonel at the roulette table. They went to the Colonel's room, where they exchanged a million-dollar check for a handshake to be Elvis's event promoter.

After putting the cashier's check in the safe, the Colonel said, "Do you want to meet Elvis?" He was staying in the room next door. When the door opened and Elvis came forward, the Colonel said, "This is the young man who's going to take you back on the road."

With his Southern hospitality, Elvis said, "I look forward to it. I have two simple rules: #1, I will only sing to a sold-out crowd; #2, I only want my fans on the front row. I don't want people who paid high ticket prices. I want my fans. Can you promise me that?"

Not wanting to disappoint the King, Jerry agreed. At times, Validators will overcommit to earn the acceptance, praise, trust, and respect they want.

### *Superpower vs. Kryptonite (Strengths vs. Weaknesses)*

Validators are great at building confidence in themselves, as well as making other people feel important. When not in check, that can backfire on them. This is their superpower and their kryptonite.

Before the Renatus National Awards Banquet, the lobby fills with excitement and anticipation. People are dressed to the nines and begin to wonder, "Is this the year I get *the award?*" The ballroom doors open promptly at 6 p.m., and 1,200 people rush to their assigned tables.

Renatus owner and CEO Bob Snyder is about to give out awards to his independent salespeople. To call it an awards banquet is to call a Learjet a commuter plane. This annual celebration would make the Oscars look like a kid's tea party.

Mr. Snyder, a Validator, travels the world, inspiring and training his more than 10,000 sales associates. When traveling, he is constantly thinking of gifts for the banquet. Each award given is customized to the individual. The event starts at 6:00 p.m., and in the last seven years it has not ended before 1:30 a.m.

On average, Snyder gives away more than 600 different awards. You would think that most people would clear out after receiving their recognition, but the culture Snyder has created throughout his company is one of team building and support. Everyone cheers and applauds for everyone else.

This culture of recognition doesn't just happen once a year at the national convention; there are also regional events, where each major market puts on a miniature version of the awards banquet. The leaders follow their CEO's example by building and crafting custom awards to recognize those who have been top performers in their field.

You would think it stops there, but it doesn't. On Super Saturdays, once a month in the individual markets, leaders take the time to acknowledge those who have made a difference in the local community.

Validators are cheerleaders. They want to acknowledge individuals who have made an impact on the team. They are driven to give praise, recognize others, and be respectful, and they are very accepting. Their currency is trust and respect.

Speaking of currency, people tend to not be as focused on money as you may think. Contrary to popular belief, employees are not primarily concerned about their company's ROI. Based on a recent study, employers still hold a false belief that eighty-nine percent of their employees leave because of pay. The reality is that people leave their bosses, not their jobs.

Those who are in management positions as Validators work on a different ROI: a "return on importance." They spend their time making other people feel important. According to an independent survey of 19,700 post-exiting employees, the number one reason they left was they felt unrecognized.

A Validator's superpower is their ability to recognize and validate others. The question is whether it can be profitable for a company to go out of its way to validate its employees. Just ask Southwest Airlines founder Herb Kelleher, a Validator. Independent research company Total Resource Network said the following after reviewing Southwest's financials:

> TRN congratulates Southwest Airlines for thirty-eight years of consecutive profitability. This is a major accomplishment that should be applauded, especially during this economic recession [in 2010] and recovery period. Southwest's success has been attributed to their core values and mission, which begin with their employees and exceptional customer service.

Profitability comes from the culture Kelleher created. Southwest's culture of making other people feel important permeates throughout the entire company, from their warrior heart logo to their stock symbol: LUV.

Carlos E. Santa Maria / Shutterstock.com

On Boss's Day 1994, Southwest Airline's 16,000 employees raised $60,000 to run a full-page ad in *USA Today*. In it, they thanked their CEO, Herb Kelleher, for his efforts.

The ad read:

> Thanks Herb,
> For remembering every one of our names.
> For supporting the Ronald McDonald House.
> For helping load baggage on Thanksgiving.
> For giving everyone a kiss (and we mean everyone).
> For listening.
> For running the only profitable major airline.
> For singing at our holiday party.
> For singing only once a year.
> For letting us wear shorts and sneakers to work.
> For golfing at the LUV Classic with only one club.
> For outtalking Sam Donaldson.
> For riding your Harley Davidson into Southwest headquarters.
> For being a friend, not just a boss.
> Happy Boss's Day from Each One of Your 16,000 Employees.

A Validator's superpower is their ability to make others feel important through praise, respect, trust, and validation. Their superpower turns to kryptonite when they shift the focus from giving these positive attributes to others to wanting them for themselves. They can become needy, untrusting, cynical about others' success, and get frustrated when people don't respect, accept, and trust them.

Let's look at President Trump, who has experienced both the strength and weakness of being a Validator. In his early career, being a Validator gave him confidence as he trusted his gut in investments, recognized his own abilities, and validated others to create the Trump brand. That same validation served him well as he ended the 1990s roughly $1 billion in debt from the recession.

He bounced back by tapping into his DRIVE and believing in himself when no one else did. He became an example of business ingenuity and perseverance.

Fast forward a couple decades, regardless of your political affiliation, and you will notice Trump's status as Validator is an incredible weakness. If you were President of the United States, would you really Tweet and pick fights with athletes, actors, and musicians? Or take up a personal vendetta with America's top news agencies, calling them "fake news"? Or create economic sanctions against other countries that will only end up hurting financially the very people who put you in office? When a Validator looks for external validation, their superpower turns into kryptonite.

## *How to Sell to a Validator* (V)

Each DRIVE has seven associated keywords. On social media or in your advertisements, you can target specific DRIVEs when you use those keywords. In future chapters, we will go into greater detail for each keyword. But for now, here is a quick snapshot. When selling to a Validator, make sure the benefits of your product or service helps them to:

- Be **trusted**
- Receive **praise**
- Be **respected**
- Receive **recognition**
- Feel **accepted**
- Be **validated**
- Be **needed**

## Executive

Left, left, right. Welterweight champion Carlos Baldomir was using Floyd "Money" Mayweather's face as a punching bag. The crowd was going crazy. It was the twelfth round, and over 400 punches had been thrown at him—some connecting and causing very real pain.

At some point, Mayweather sprained his right hand defending himself. By the twelfth round, he was using his non-dominant hand to fend off Baldomir. As the bell rang and the audience was divided between boos and cheers, the judges awarded Mayweather his thirty-seventh undefeated title.

Like Mayweather, Executives will go up against insurmountable odds to win. Executives are primarily motivated and influenced by *Proof.* They achieve this through three core channels:

- **Winning** and **control**
- **Work, providing,** and **security**
- **Problem-solving** and achieving their **goals**

Their confidence stems from getting things done and feeling successful. They are motivated to win and to be in control.

Every year from 2009–2018, Floyd Mayweather was among the highest-paid athletes in the world. In 2018, he earned $285 million—$174 million more than the second-highest-paid athlete (Lionel Messi).

Perhaps even more impressive is that Floyd has earned over $1 billion in career earnings without a single meaningful endorsement deal. He is the first and only athlete to exceed a billion from actual earnings. Michael Jordan (Executive) and Tiger Woods (Executive) are the only other two athletes to cross the billion-dollar mark with a combination of salary and endorsements.

Between 1996–2006, Floyd was represented by Bob Arum's Top Rank Boxing promotional company (Top Rank has promoted boxing's elite, such as Muhammad Ali, Oscar De La Hoya, and Manny Pacquiao).

In boxing, when you are signed with a promoter, you basically become an employee. You are offered a set amount of money to appear at a fight. The promoter puts up all the money and takes on all the risk to organize the fight. By taking on the risk, the promoter also reaps the biggest rewards. Any profits left over after costs have been paid (including the cost to pay the fighters) go straight into Bob Arum's pockets.

In April 2006, Bob Arum offered Floyd $8 million to fight Antonio Margarito. That would have doubled Floyd's previous highest purse. Floyd, being an Executive, did not feel as if he was in control; he didn't have security, and he certainly wasn't winning financially.

He wanted $20 million to fight Oscar De La Hoya. Arum was stunned and didn't think that amount of money for Floyd to fight Oscar would pay off. So, he declined and kept pushing the Margarito bout instead.

One of the strengths of an Executive is problem-solving. To take control of his career, Floyd decided to buy out his contract with Arum. He paid him $750,000, then opened Mayweather Promotions.

He got his fight with De La Hoya. It took place in May 2007. The bout smashed the record for pay-per-view buys—$2.5 million. After paying all the costs, Mayweather took home $25 million. At the time, it was the highest revenue-producing fight in boxing history.

Today, Floyd fronts all the money for an event, including his opponent's purse. With the famous Conor McGregor fight, Floyd fronted most of the costs to organize the event and cut McGregor a $30 million guaranteed check just to show up. When the night was over, Floyd got the majority share of the unprecedented $550 million fight—netting $275 million for a single fight.

### *Superpower vs. Kryptonite (Strengths vs. Weaknesses)*

Executives are determined to win at all costs—whether it is on the home front, with friends, or at work. This is both their superpower and their kryptonite.

The air smelled of high-octane fuel from the bleachers to the paddocks. The crowd was screaming as thunderous race cars passed the pits at full speed. As the checkered flag fell at Sebring raceway, first, second, and third were all Ferraris.

*I need those red cars,* Henry Ford II (Executive) thought.

Ford wanted the world to know his company was capable of racing. In 1957, the Automobile Manufacturers of America declared that all manufacturers in the group could not participate in any forms of motorsport. Ford was the chairman of the group, and took this commitment seriously.

So, he was furious to find out that Chevrolet had ignored the entire rule and built a new race car called the Corvette. Wanting to win, and being years behind in development, he thought it would be quicker to buy a racing company than to build one from scratch.

At the time, the Europeans were dominating the racetrack, with prominent names such as Porsche, Alfa Romeo, and Ferrari pulling in all the wins. Ford planned to purchase one of these marquee brands in order to give a massive head start to their new racing program.

© Stuart Hickling / Alamy Stock Photo

At the time, Ferrari was the powerhouse in the grueling twenty-four-hour Le Mans race, with their striking Ferrari 330 P3 easily winning the title. Ford decided to buy Ferrari because of their dominance at Le Mans. Ferrari's founder and CEO, Enzo Ferrari (Executive), was keen on selling his company, with an agreed amount of $15 million. Ford traveled to Italy and spent several million dollars auditing Ferrari.

When Enzo read through the contract, he noticed a small detail he did not expect—one that would affect his company in a lasting and permanent way. The contract stated Ford would take over both Ferrari's racing and automotive division. Enzo exploded and underlined the lines with purple ink. Next to them, he scribbled "unacceptable," before hurling a string of insults at Ford executives.

Fuming with anger, Ford gathered his top executives into a conference and gave them an unequivocal command: "Go to Le Mans, and beat Ferrari's ass."

Executives do not like to take second. And now two Executives were about to go head-to-head for first place.

Enzo Ferrari wanted to teach Ford a lesson by redesigning the 330 P3. It was the new shining star of the brand, a dominating

V12-powered, beautifully designed, aerodynamic, and innovative racing prototype, implementing technologies such as fuel injection and a custom-made gearbox to maintain its ongoing dominance at Le Mans.

Ferrari's P series had secured Ferrari six wins by the end of 1963—the most wins achieved by an auto manufacturer at the time.

Meanwhile, across the pond, Ford was still developing its first car to race at Le Mans. On April 1, 1964, Ford's Ferrari-killer was unveiled to the world. Ford was truly proud of what they had achieved. Sadly, the Ford GT40 was a huge embarrassment; all three cars were retired after just two laps around the circuit. Meanwhile, Ferrari had once again taken the title for championship at Le Mans.

Executives want control. Ford hired legendary automotive genius Carrol Shelby to help him rebuild the GT40. To increase his chances of winning, Ford poached Ferrari's head engineer, compensating him with a house, car, university for his children, and three times the salary he was making. Enzo retaliated by poaching Ford's highest winning driver, Bob Bondurant.

Race day arrived—the race that Ford had dreamt of beating Ferrari. Ford's chance for victory had come, after years of humiliation by Ferrari, along with its biggest opportunity to put its name in the racing history books, letting the world know Ford was truly capable of winning.

The race began at noon. The leading car fluctuated between the new Ford GT40 and the Ferrari 330 P4. At the end of the first hour, Ford had dominated the race, leading in the first three positions by a massive twenty-four seconds.

At dusk, Ferrari took the lead, with Ford fighting to catch up from behind. However, due to massive rainfall, two Ferrari 330s that were behind had spun and crashed, leaving only the leading 330 left.

As of sunrise, Ferrari had maintained lead position. One of the Ford GT40s had crashed as a result of slipping due to spilled gas. The lead Ferrari kept the pursuit on full tilt until the moment that would turn the tables for the entire race.

The leading Ferrari 330 P3 had blown a tire, marking the entire team as DNF (did not finish). After trailing behind the Ferrari for so long, the GT40 overtook it and led the race till the end.

© GP Library Limited / Alamy Stock Photo

Ford beat Ferrari in the biggest way possible, as the Ford GT40 took the top three positions at Le Mans, while none of the Ferraris had even finished the race. All that hard work Ford's racing development team had put into the project had finally paid off.

After 1966, Ford continued to maintain its title as champion and dominated Le Mans from 1966–1969. Ferrari would never again win at Le Mans. Ford beat Ferrari not only in Le Mans, but throughout the entire International Prototype Sports Cars from 1966–1968. They kept on winning in races such as Daytona, Sebring, and Spa, winning the champion manufacturer title three times.

In business, Executives do not like to lose. They do not want to fall behind or lose their competitive edge. This drive to win sometimes becomes their kryptonite. They are so thirsty to get ahead and have control that they accidentally alienate their customer base, employees, and investors.

In the 1980s, Pepsi launched a new ad campaign called "The Pepsi Generation." It was the first time Pepsi outsold Coca Cola during their ninety-year battle for supremacy. Not to be outdone, the executives at

Coca Cola introduced "New Coke." On April 23, 1985, New Coke was launched to much fanfare, including prime time TV ads.

Company chairman Roberto C. Goizueta proclaimed New Coke "smoother, rounder, yet bolder," speaking of it more like a fine wine than a soda. What the company didn't estimate was the enormous backlash.

MSNBC reported, "Public reaction was overwhelmingly negative; some people likened the change in Coke to trampling the American flag." Within four short months, after investing tens of millions of dollars, Coca-Cola pulled the product from the shelves.

Of the debacle, company President Donald R. Keough said, "We did not understand the deep emotions of so many of our customers for Coca-Cola." Sam Craig, marketing professor, along with other industry observers viewed the biggest mistake on Coca-Cola's part was that, "They didn't ask the critical question of Coke users: 'Do you *want* a new Coke?'" They never asked the questions because they were so focused on winning and not losing to Pepsi.

## *How to Sell to an Executive*

E

Each DRIVE has seven associated keywords. On social media or in your advertisements, you can target specific DRIVEs when you use those keywords. In future chapters, we will go into greater detail for each keyword. But for now, here is a quick snapshot. When selling to an Executive, make sure the benefits of your product or service helps them to:

- Feel like they are **winning**
- Have a sense of **control**
- Have success in their **work**
- Reach their **goals**
- Feel a sense of **security**
- **Provide** for the people they choose
- **Solve problems**

4

# Why vs. How

*I cannot believe I am on the verge of bankruptcy. Never in my wildest imagination did I think I would be where I am today.* These thoughts and many worse swirled around his head as a middle-aged man sat on a bench in New York's spacious Central Park. He was deep in debt and could see no way out. Business creditors were closing in on him. Suppliers were demanding payment. He sat head in hands, wondering if anything could save his company from bankruptcy.

Suddenly, an old man appeared before him. "I can see that something is troubling you," he said. After listening to the executive's woes, the old man said, "I believe I can help you." He asked the man his name, wrote out a check, and pushed it into his hand, saying, "Take this money. Meet me here exactly one year from today, and you can pay me back at that time." Then he turned and disappeared as quickly as he had come.

The business executive saw in his hand a check for $500,000, signed by John D. Rockefeller, then one of the richest men in the world!

"I can erase my money worries in an instant!" he realized. But instead, the executive decided to put the uncashed check in his safe. *Just knowing it's there might give me the strength to work out a way to save my business,* he thought. With renewed optimism, he negotiated better deals and extended terms of payment. He closed several big sales. Within a few months, he was out of debt and making money once again.

Exactly one year later, he returned to the park with the uncashed check. At the agreed-upon time, the old man appeared. Just as the executive was about to hand back the check and share his success story, a nurse came running up and grabbed the old man.

"I'm so glad I caught him!" she cried. "I hope he hasn't been bothering you. He's always escaping from the rest home and telling people he's John D. Rockefeller." And she led the old man away by the arm.

The astonished executive just stood there, stunned. All year long he'd been wheeling and dealing, buying and selling, convinced that he had half a million dollars behind him. Suddenly, he realized that it wasn't the money, real or imagined, that had turned his life around. It was his newfound self-confidence that gave him the power to achieve anything he went after.

As a sales professional, *confidence* fuels you to press forward when everything seems impossible. There is a way to tap into unlimited fuel—to give you the confidence you need when your back is against the wall. It is your secondary DRIVE.

The first DRIVE you chose is based on what makes you *feel* important. It is the lead actor in this play called life. The second DRIVE you chose is your supporting cast. Your primary DRIVE is *why* you do what you do (your motive). The secondary DRIVE is *how* you go about it (your process). This concept is key, so let's look back at Walt Disney to see how it plays out in real life.

Walt Disney's primary DRIVE was a Director, so he was motivated by *Lifestyle*. Examine the layout of Disneyland: it has Main Street, USA, Frontierland, Tomorrowland, Fantasyland, Critter Country, New Orleans Square, Mickey's Toon Town, and now Star Wars: Galaxy's Edge.

On those eighty-five acres of Disneyland, you can experience everything from Main Street to a galaxy far, far away. Walt's motivation was to create an experience for everyday folks to come into his magic kingdom and be transported to different times and places. That is *why* Disneyland was designed around Walt's DRIVE.

*How* he accomplished it, however, was through his secondary DRIVE, Relator—which is driven by *Community*. Disney surrounded himself with a small group of animators affectionately referred to as

Disney's "Nine Old Men." They were there from the beginning of Snow White, and through their loyalty spent their entire careers at the studio. To immortalize his friendship with them, he painted their names on the shop windows on Main Street.

Before Disneyland was built, Walt faced a real conundrum: how to fund a family theme park. It had never been done before. Meetings with investors proved fruitless. Roy Disney was scheduled to fly to New York to pitch ABC to invest in the park in forty-eight hours.

Walt called Herb Ryman, a Disney artist, and told him how he was going to build this magical theme park. He went into great detail, describing the castle with a moat, the Matterhorn with a rollercoaster in the middle, and the jungle cruise with animatronic animals. As Herb listened, he continued to get more and more excited.

He finally said, "I cannot wait to see the drawings!"

"See the drawings?" replied Walt. "There are no drawings, Herb. I need you to draw my vision." For the next forty-eight hours, Walt stood over Herb's shoulders and described every detail of the park.

A decade later when Walt was on his deathbed, he turned to his lifelong business partner and brother Roy Disney. Walt begged him to finish his dream. Roy postponed his retirement and promised him that he would complete his vision of Disney World. As a Director, Walt was a visionary. But he accomplished his dreams through his secondary DRIVE, Relator, by turning to *Community*.

Here's another way to look at it: Your primary DRIVE is the car, and the fuel is your secondary DRIVE. When your tank is full, you can reach your destination. When your tank is empty, you are stuck. Take a moment and analyze your DRIVE. Examine your primary DRIVE and then look at your secondary DRIVE; you will notice your *why* versus your *how*.

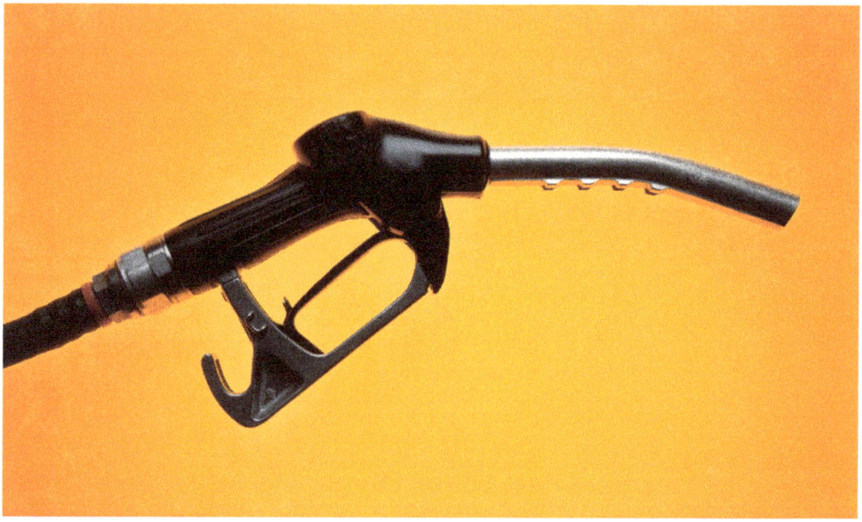

- Do you experience frustration when your secondary DRIVE is not being met?
- As you reflect on your life, do you notice that you feel most confident when your secondary DRIVE is fueling your primary DRIVE?
- Do you feel fearful when your secondary DRIVE is not supporting your primary?

- Do successes in your life, relationships, and business come when your secondary DRIVE is being validated and fueling your primary DRIVE?

Knowing how your secondary DRIVE affects you will help you tap into your superpower and navigate key relationships in a way you never have before. Just for fun, interview someone's DRIVE who is close to you (see Chapter 1). Analyze their secondary DRIVE and see how it has impacted their decision making, lifestyle, and relationships.

Interview your spouse, significant other, business partner, parents, siblings, or best friend. Make sure it is someone you know well. As you see their secondary DRIVE and how it has influenced them, you will also see how it has impacted you and your relationship with them.

This exercise is crucial to closing more sales. Mastering your secondary DRIVE gives you more determination and ambition to sell. It also helps you bounce back from rejection and the emotional roller coaster of being a professional salesperson.

In my own business, knowing my secondary DRIVE has saved me more times than I can count. Due to a scheduling conflict, I lost two six-figure speaking gigs one year. Based on the previous year's sales from those same events, I lost a potential $750,000. Needless to say, I was leveled emotionally for a little bit.

Knowing the role of my secondary DRIVE, I consciously chose to invest in my Relator DRIVE. I called everyone I knew who specialized in my type of business as a speaker, author, and business strategist. What I learned from them and the opportunities that came from those calls would far exceed the loss.

Here are a few examples of successful individuals and how they used their secondary DRIVE to fuel their primary DRIVE to reach unprecedented success. For now, just skip to your secondary DRIVE and read that story, then move on to the next chapter; you can always come back and read the others.

## Secondary DRIVE

## Floyd Mayweather—
## Professional Boxer / Promoter

*Primary DRIVE (Why): Executive = Proof*

*Secondary DRIVE (How): Director = Lifestyle*

Floyd's rise to absolute financial dominance in the world of sports never would have happened without his secondary DRIVE— Director. It started with one very simple decision he made back in 2006, while standing at the crossroads of his career.

Should he stay with Bob Arum's Top Rank Boxing and take his guaranteed $8 million purse to fight Antonio Margarito or risk it all to buy out his contract, put up the money to fight Oscar De La Hoya, and potentially lose his undefeated title as well as all of his money?

Without this secondary DRIVE, Floyd would not have taken the risk. With a primary DRIVE of Executive, his *why* is to win and have control. To achieve this, he relies on his secondary DRIVE of Director (the *how*) to be free and independent as well as to find a creative solution.

The fight with De La Hoya smashed the record for pay-per-view buys: 2.5 million. After paying all the costs, Mayweather took home a cool $25 million. Without his secondary DRIVE, he wouldn't have found a way to buy back his contract and have the courage to take the risk with De La Hoya.

MAYWEATHER
PROMOTIONS

His Director DRIVE continued to help him as he went on to fight Saul Alvarez in 2013, netting him $75 million. Feeling free and independent to do any fight he wanted, Mayweather took on Conor McGregor—and after winning, took home $275 million.

When Mayweather was under Bob Arum, his ten-year career earnings were $10 million. When he relied on his secondary DRIVE and opened

Mayweather Promotions, his career earnings skyrocketed to over $1 billion.

If your secondary DRIVE is Director, answer the following question (otherwise skip):

- Do you use any of the following to meet your primary DRIVE: creativity, freedom and independence, life's purpose, appearance, performing, experiencing life, or overcoming challenges?

Remember, your primary DRIVE is the car and the secondary is the fuel. When you get stuck and feel like you can't move forward, you need to fuel up by investing in your secondary DRIVE. To increase your confidence and give you courage to fulfill your true potential, here are ten activities you can do to support your Secondary DRIVE.

### D DIRECTOR—Fuel *(Secondary DRIVE)*

- Travel
- Experience something new
- Play, play, play
- Write a personal Declaration of Independence
- Start a new hobby
- Study the lives of other great people
- Listen to music
- Acknowledge your triumphs
- Volunteer in your expertise
- Clarify your purpose

With your primary and secondary DRIVE intact, you are now ready to learn how to increase your sales potential by 400 percent.

## Sir Richard Branson—Founder of the Virgin Group

*Primary DRIVE (Why): Director = Lifestyle*

*Secondary DRIVE (How): Relator = Community*

Whether Richard Branson was dropping out of high school, launching Virgin Records, buying an island, or building an international airline, his motive as a Director (primary) was to have the *Lifestyle* he wanted. This was *why* he did what he did. However, *how* he was able to do the impossible was through his secondary DRIVE—Relator.

When he launched Virgin Records, Richard's relationships drove its success. His first signed artist was Mike Oldfield, with his album *Tubular Bells*. The album would go on to worldwide success, selling fifteen million copies. But it almost didn't happen.

Mike's first concert was sold out. The press and music insiders gathered at Queen Elizabeth Hall on June 25, 1973. TV crews were setting up as audience members stood in line. Mike visited Richard on his houseboat and in a deathly whisper said, "I cannot go through with the concert tonight."

Even though Mick Taylor, the guitarist from the Rolling Stones, was going to accompany him on stage, he was resolved to not perform. Richard knew that pressuring him would not help. He said, "Let's go for a drive."

Mike had always admired Branson's Bentley. Branson tossed him the keys, and Mike slid into the faded red seats. They passed the concert hall, where the large Mike Oldfield banners hung, proclaiming "Live in Concert Tonight."

They continued to drive. Nothing Richard said helped calm Mike down. He was in full panic mode. Richard turned to Mike and said, "Would you like to have this car as a present?"

"A present?!" Mike replied.

"Yes. I'll get out here and walk home. You just keep on driving, and the car is yours," said Branson.

"Come off it! It was your wedding present from your parents," Mike responded.

"All you have to do is drive it around to Queen Elizabeth Hall and go up on stage tonight, and it's yours."

Silence fell between them as Mike gripped the steering wheel, imagining driving around town in a Bentley. "It's a deal."

As the concert came to an end, the audience leapt to their feet with a thunderous standing ovation. Branson and his wife Kristen walked home. He relied on his secondary DRIVE as a Relator. He figured he could explain to his wife and parents that he leveraged the car to save his business.

After the success of *Tubular Bells*, Branson owed Oldfield his next royalty payment. Virgin Records was in a heavy acquisition stage by signing up new talent, and Branson did not have the funds to pay Oldfield and his new artist. Relying on his relationships, he went to Mike and said, "I am sorry I cannot pay you what I owe you. And could I borrow a million dollars to be able to sign Madonna?"

Mike didn't flinch. He loaned Branson the money. Without his deep-rooted relationships, he never would be able to fund his Director *Lifestyle.*

If your secondary DRIVE is a Relator, answer the following question (otherwise skip):

- Do you use relationships, influence, service, family, friends, parenting, or spirituality to meet your primary DRIVE?

Remember, your primary DRIVE is the car and the secondary is the fuel. When you get stuck and feel like you can't move forward, you need to fuel up by investing in your secondary DRIVE. To increase your confidence and give you courage to fulfill your true potential, here are ten activities you can do to support your Secondary DRIVE.

## RELATOR—Fuel *(Secondary DRIVE)* R

- Anonymously serve
- List your gratitude
- Pray or meditate
- Pamper yourself
- Celebrate with close friends
- Join a networking group
- Keep a journal
- Send thank-you notes
- Forgive someone
- Let go of grudges, anger, and negative thoughts

With your primary and secondary DRIVE intact, you are now ready to learn how to increase your sales potential by 400 percent.

## Jerry Weintraub—
## Event Promoter / Hollywood Producer

*Primary Drive (Why) Validator = Admiration*

*Secondary DRIVE (How) Intellectual = System*

How does a no-name event promoter get the attention of the King? It was Weintraub's secondary DRIVE (Intellectual) that gave him the fuel to be a success. Elvis's manager told Jerry, "Since I have never heard of you, I assume you are a nobody and therefore I am not interested." That would have destroyed anyone with a primary DRIVE of Validator—but not with a secondary DRIVE of Intellectual.

Intellectuals are motivated by creating systems. Instead of feeling offended as a Validator, he created a phone tree *System* to raise the money. Your secondary DRIVE is where you find the strength to push on when everything seems lost. If you invest in your secondary DRIVE, you will go to levels you have not yet experienced.

Weintraub's first concert with Elvis was in Miami Beach, Florida, on the Fourth of July. When the crew and Jerry arrived twenty-four hours

Phillip Harrington / Alamy Stock Photo

before the concert for the soundcheck, he was shocked at what he saw. "Are those tickets for Will Call?" he inquired. "No," said the manager, "those 5,000 tickets are for the matinée show that we didn't sell."

When Elvis had given Jerry the opportunity to promote him, one of the requirements was he would only sing to sold-out shows. Jerry grabbed the manager by the collar and screamed, "You said it was sold out!"

"I only told you what you wanted to hear," the manager calmly replied. Weintraub rushed to the Colonel and said, "We have a problem. We have 5,000 tickets left for the matinée." The Colonel replied, "*We* don't have a problem, son. *You* do."

In times of challenges, the secondary DRIVE really begins to show its value, as it did for Jerry on this fateful day. Relying on his Intellectual DRIVE, he ran across the street to the Dade County Sheriff's Office with a bag full of money and convinced the sheriff to let him hire inmates to unscrew 5,000 seats from the auditorium and put them in the parking lot under a large blue tarp.

The next day, Elvis did perform to a sold-out matinée. After the show, the inmates put the seats back in the auditorium for the sold-out evening show. Later that night, after the show, Elvis turned to Jerry and said, "You know what? We should think carefully about the matinées; the audience is much louder and grand in the evenings." Jerry agreed.

Weintraub would go on to have a very successful career, promoting legends from Elvis to Frank Sinatra. Taking his organizational skill-set to Hollywood, he produced movies including the *Karate Kid* and *Oceans 11*, *Oceans 12*, and *Oceans 13*. By using his secondary DRIVE as an Intellectual, he was able to make his dream about his name and Elvis's name together on the marquee of Madison Square Garden a reality.

If your secondary DRIVE is an Intellectual, answer the following question (otherwise skip):

- Do you use any of the following to meet your primary DRIVE: learning, knowledge, health, nature, being in the moment, standards, or organization?

Remember, your primary DRIVE is the car and the secondary is the fuel. When you get stuck and feel like you can't move forward, you need to fuel up by investing in your secondary DRIVE. To increase your confidence and give you courage to fulfill your true potential, here are ten activities you can do to support your Secondary DRIVE.

## I INTELLECTUAL—Fuel *(Secondary DRIVE)*

- Organize your schedule
- Say no to ineffective offers
- Learn something new
- Live with integrity
- Create a system for your business, family, or life
- Hike, bike, or just get outside
- Join a book club

- Pick a new topic to study
- Schedule time for your fitness
- Take an online course

With your primary and secondary DRIVE intact, you are now ready to learn how to increase your sales potential by 400 percent.

## Fred Smith— Founder of FedEx

*Primary Drive (Why) Intellectual = System*

V *Secondary DRIVE (How) Validator = Admiration*

How crazy do you have to be to take your company's last $5,000 and head to Las Vegas to bet it all to make payroll within seventy-two hours? Is it crazy, or just the right amount of confidence?

Fred Smith, the founder of FedEx, is an Intellectual (primary). He is motivated to build systems and make things more efficient. This is how he created FedEx, even though the U.S. Postal Service and UPS had already been in business for decades. Being an Intellectual is *why* he does what he does. His secondary DRIVE—Validator—is *how* he goes about it.

Validators believe in themselves. When Fred's college professor gave him his grade for his central hub shipping term paper with the comment, "The concept is interesting and well-formed, but in order to earn better than a C, the idea must be feasible," it was his secondary DRIVE (Validator) that gave him the courage to believe he could make it happen.

After returning from Vietnam, Smith had devised a well-thought-out strategy to implement his idea while making the most of his resources. Originally, Smith wanted to do contract work for the Federal Reserve System, transporting, sorting, and rerouting checks. His business plan called for a fleet of planes that would pick up packages for delivery. The planes and cargo would be flown at night, when air traffic was minimal; packages would then be dropped at a central location or hub, where they would be sorted.

From there, the parcels, using both ground and air, would be routed to their destinations within twenty-four hours. Smith chose Memphis as the hub city because of its central location, moderate climate, and labor resources. Smith also wanted the company to own its own planes in order to bypass federal shipping regulations.

Despite Smith's proposals, which he calculated would have saved the nation's banking system an estimated $3 million a day, many financial institutions were not convinced that Smith's ideas could realistically be carried out.

On paper, Smith's delivery system was simple and practical. However, there were many problems to overcome to make it work. Financially, the business required a tremendous amount of money for planes, pilots, and insurance. Smith also needed to design a transportation system that could not only link any two parts of the country but also ensure that packages going back and forth could be delivered within the promised twenty-four-hour window—something that had never been tried before in cargo delivery.

Bank after bank turned him down. At this point, an average entrepreneur would concede and give up. It was Smith's secondary DRIVE (Validator) that fueled his determination. He raised $92 million and added it to his $4 million inheritance left by his father to invest in his unproven system.

When the money ran out and his sisters sued him for inappropriate use of funds, most people would have stopped there. Only a secondary DRIVE of Validator would give him the confidence to believe and double down on himself.

When he could not raise any more money from investors, he didn't fly home and quit. He boarded a plane to Las Vegas and spent the next forty-eight hours at the blackjack table, gambling his company's last $5,000 to make payroll by Monday.

As the corporate executives came into the office, they expected to see the business in shambles. Instead, Smith was revitalized with his earnings, and they were able to make payroll. Within a week, they raised $11 million to not only save the company but launch it into the stratosphere, becoming the first American company to gross a billion dollars in revenue.

It was his secondary DRIVE as a Validator that allowed him to believe in himself and overcome unbeatable odds when every professional and family member did not believe in him.

If your secondary DRIVE is a Validator, answer the following question (otherwise skip):

- Do you use any of the following to meet your primary DRIVE: trust, respect, acceptance, praise, validation, or recognition?

Remember, your primary DRIVE is the car and the secondary is the fuel. When you get stuck and feel like you can't move forward, you need to fuel up by investing in your secondary DRIVE. To increase your confidence and give you courage to fulfill your true potential, here are ten activities you can do to support your Secondary DRIVE.

## (V) VALIDATOR—Fuel *(Secondary DRIVE)*

- Keep a journal of your accomplishments
- Pamper yourself

- List ten things you do well
- Trust your instincts
- Accept yourself and others
- Read self-help books
- Lift someone else's burdens
- Give gratitude for all you do
- Create a shrine of success in your home office
- Give yourself permission to dream

With your primary and secondary DRIVE intact, you are now ready to learn how to increase your sales potential by 400 percent.

## Bruce Halle—
## Founder Discount Tires

*Primary DRIVE (Why): Relator = Community*

(E) *Secondary DRIVE (How) Executive = Proof*

When you think of Discount Tires, think In-N-Out Burger. Like In-N-Out, Discount only serves a handful of options. Most tire companies thrive with add-on services like alignments, brakes, mufflers, battery replacements, and oil lubes.

Not Discount. You have two choices: you can have tires or wheels. When Bruce Halle started Discount Tire, he didn't have the money to provide any additional services. As a Relator (primary) he also knew his customers would wait longer if more services were provided. However, his secondary DRIVE as an Executive is *how* he makes his business decisions.

Executives want to win, have control, provide, solve problems, work, have security, and reach their goals. In Halle's biography, *Six Tires, No Plan,* you can see how he used his analytical secondary DRIVE as an Executive to meet his primary DRIVE (Relator) to take care of his customers.

> By focusing on a limited number of services, the company can reduce customer wait times and build satisfaction. Training expense is reduced, inventory management is simplified, work scheduling is more predictable, and units per man hour can be maximized. By servicing customers faster, the stores can serve more customers per day with the same number of employees and work bays, which leverages the fixed investment in each store.

As a Relator (primary), Halle has instituted a policy to only promote from within the company. However, there are times when certain managers are not ready or qualified for advancement. Using his Executive DRIVE (secondary), Halle has implemented a Reset Button.

This is for managers who are not performing (winning, taking control, or reaching their goals) to be demoted with the chance to earn the right to be a manager again when they are qualified. Many top executives who have worked their way up the ladder have had their careers reset at one time or another. This instills in everyone that the company cares about their careers and wants them to succeed as well as protect the company's interest.

The company is driven to make customers happy. CFO Christian Rose says, "We need the customer. The customer doesn't need us." When a customer is dissatisfied, the store manager must address the issue personally. At 6 p.m. each night, every store manager receives an e-mail with the names of unhappy customers who need to be contacted within twenty-four hours. Ultimately, the managers will convert many of the dissatisfied customers into lifelong patrons simply by making a personal connection and offering to solve their problem.

Halle's secondary DRIVE (Executive) propelled this Relator from needing to sell six tires a day to become the largest tire retailer in the world. Discount Tires has a track record few companies can match. After fifty years of operation, they have never had a down year or layoffs—even though they have survived four economic recessions. Their sales exceed $4 billion, and they operate at over 1,000 locations.

Before Bruce Halle passed away, he said:

> My people are part of my family. Their health, security, their futures, that's my responsibility. We have 10,000 people working for Discount Tire, but you have to take into account they are married and have children. I am really responsible for 60,000 or 70,000 people.

As a Relator, to protect this "family," he used his Secondary DRIVE as an Executive by putting 100 percent of the company's stock into a family trust so the company could never be sold or taken public. This way, he would be able to ensure his company would pass from generation to generation and secure jobs for his extended family and his employees.

If your secondary DRIVE is an Executive, answer the following question (otherwise skip):

- Do you use any of the following to meet your primary DRIVE: winning, control, problem-solving, working, providing, security, or reaching your goals?

Remember, your primary DRIVE is the car and the secondary is the fuel. When you get stuck and feel like you can't move forward, you need to fuel up by investing in your secondary DRIVE. To increase your confidence and give you courage to fulfill your true potential, here are ten activities you can do to support your Secondary DRIVE.

## EXECUTIVE—Fuel *(Secondary DRIVE)* (E)

- Set small, obtainable goals
- Reward yourself after reaching your goals
- Stop trying to solve others' problems
- Put a plan in action
- Focus on where you are winning in your life
- Organize your work environment
- Save 10 percent of what you make
- Have an accountability partner
- Let go of what you cannot control
- Join an investment club

With your primary and secondary DRIVE intact, you are now ready to learn how to increase your sales potential by 400 percent.

20%
80%

5

# The 20/80 Rule

Do you want to increase your sales potential by 400 percent? For over a hundred years, authors have written on influence and sales techniques. As great as some of those books have been, they still have not increased the average salesperson's twenty percent closing ratio. And here is why: if the greatest salesperson in the world who only speaks English is sent to the Orient to sell, they are going to fail. It all comes down to language. There are five buying languages. You speak one, which equals twenty percent. When you master the other four languages, you have the potential to increase your sales by 400 percent.

The 20/80 Rule states, "You lose eighty percent of sales based on your DRIVE." When you sell, you are selling from your DRIVE and alienating the other four DRIVEs, which are eighty percent. Have you ever walked out of a sales presentation, felt you crushed it, and then never received a return call from your potential client?

If you have, it is because you spoke your DRIVE and were completely stimulated, but your potential clients were turned off. The opposite is also true: have you ever been presented an opportunity and were instantly turned off? That is because the salesperson was not speaking your DRIVE language. Therefore, you were not motivated to buy.

My wife and I had just finished our backyard, and we always wanted a hot tub to sit out and enjoy the views of the golf course, lake, and mountains. We designed our patio to take full advantage of the spectacular scenery. Everything was in place, from the newly-poured concrete to the electricity being hooked up. All we needed now was the hot tub.

With the kids in tow, we headed off to get our long-awaited prize. After looking around a bit and having the kids climb in and out of each one, testing its size and comfort, a tall, well-informed salesman approached us. Being a Director, I was ready to buy our new hot tub on the spot and get it home so we could start enjoying ourselves.

Sadly, the salesman, an Intellectual, spent the next twenty minutes describing the one-piece fiberglass mold, the interchangeable jets, the electrical wiring of the machine, how many years he had worked for the company, and how their system was stronger and better than any other competitor. We were bored out of our minds. If he would have just asked, "What inspired you to want to get a hot tub?" and then just sold us based on my answer, we would have bought it in less than five minutes.

Instead, we were so turned off by his intellectual sales approach that we walked away. Six months later, we still have a blank piece of concrete in the backyard yearning to be covered with a hot tub. The way he was selling was as an Intellectual, which is only twenty percent of DRIVE. By doing this, he alienated the other four personalities: Directors, Relators, Validators, and Executives.

In the Introduction, we briefly covered the 20/80 Rule and the reason why Walt Disney could not inspire Art Linkletter to buy the property surrounding what would become Disneyland. Disney, a Director, was trying to influence Linkletter with what would only appeal to a Director. Linkletter was a Validator, motivated by Admiration.

No matter what Disney said, it meant nothing to Linkletter. Buying land next to Disneyland did not bring him any validation, and therefore he passed, even though they were dear friends and Linkletter was the master of ceremonies on Disneyland's opening day. The Fujishige family (Executives) saw the opportunity as a good investment and bought fifty-six acres across the street for $2,500. In the late 90s, they sold it back to the Disney Corporation for just under $100 million.

When Broncos owner Pat Bowlen, an Intellectual, pitched John Elway, a Director, it failed, but not because Elway couldn't afford it or didn't love the Broncos. Elway spent his entire NFL career with the Broncos and continued to work with them as President/CEO. And he was flush with cash from selling his car dealership. So, money was not the problem, the relationship was not the issue, and brand loyalty was not wanting. Elway had a financial guarantee and still did not invest. Why would someone not buy even after being the face and image of the brand? The only answer is Bowlen did not speak the buying language Elway needed to trigger the desire to invest.

Companies do this every day and don't know it. They accidentally market to only one DRIVE and alienate the others. In the mid-1800s, two Intellectuals, Antoni Patek and Adrien Philippe, invented and patented some of the most advanced watches for the day. These included the first keyless winding system, the first Swiss wristwatch, and the world's first split-second chronograph wristwatch.

Their watches were coveted and collected by royalty and celebrities alike. When Albert Einstein, an Intellectual, wanted to celebrate the discovery of the Theory of General Relativity, he bought a Patek Philippe. For 100 years, they continued to innovate and create ground-breaking watches.

In 1932, Charles and Jean Stern invested in and took over Patek Philippe. When the Stern family (who are Relators) got involved, they shifted from showcasing their innovations in their ads to relationship marketing. Today, it is run by fourth-generation Thierry Stern. In 1996, they launched the "Generation" ad with the tagline, "You never own a Patek Phillipe. You merely look after it for the next generation."

Their ads and commercials are focused unknowingly on attracting Relators by showing a father and son out boating or driving a classic car. Their women's watches show a mother and daughter at a ballet recital or in a ball gown with the same tagline. The 20/80 Rule applies. They are losing potentially eighty percent of sales by ignoring the Directors, Intellectuals, Validators, and Executives. When you are selling a $25,000 watch, it would be wise to not distance yourself from eighty percent of the market.

You may be surprised to see the 20/80 also applies in the Shark Tank.

*Shark Tank Closing Stats*

| Name | Times Pitched | Deals Closed | Closing Ratio |
|---|---|---|---|
| Robert Herjavec | 511 | 57 | 11% |
| Lori Greiner | 311 | 61 | 19% |
| Daymond John | 407 | 61 | 15% |
| Mark Cuban | 403 | 85 | 19% |
| Kevin O'Leary | 531 | 40 | 8% |

When you examine these numbers, an interesting fact is that Kevin O'Leary, an Executive, has been pitched the most out of all the sharks, but he has done the least amount of deals. It isn't surprising when you understand that as an Executive, O'Leary requires the most amount of proof before making a decision.

This is why one of his leading questions when grilling contestants is, "Do you have any sales? What are your numbers?" When you are selling to an Executive, you need to have Proof. When you look at O'Leary's top investments, he spent 2.5 times more on his largest investment compared to his second largest all because of proof. He invested $2,500,000 into Zipz, which owns the patent for the clear film used to protect individual glasses of wine.

What is one of the most profitable industries? As you examine the safest and most profitable industry for an Executive to put their money in, it would have to be wine and spirits. When selling to an Executive, your sales numbers have to be accurate and verified. If you can, provide third-party testimonials. Focus on the big picture, not the details, until they ask for them. If your product or services address these issues, you will have success with Executives.

Mark Cuban, a Validator, has been pitched the second least amount of times but has done the most deals. Why? Could it be that as a Validator he gets attention and admiration when saying yes? His largest investment was $2,000,000 into Ten Thirty One Productions for a ten percent stake. Ten Thirty One Productions is a party company. Mr. Validator bought a party company to be the life of the party. If you are selling to a Validator, make sure your product or service is going to make them look good. Is your product going to help them shine at work or at home? Is it going to support them in their life? If your product or service addresses these issues, you will have success with Validators.

Robert Herjavec, a Director, is driven to invest in businesses that are lifestyle-based, whether they involve motorized surfboards, kayaks, novelty footwear, or custom golf putters. To defend his DRIVE, his largest investment was $5,000,000 into a car company called Zero Pollution Motors for fifty percent of their business. The cars run on compressed air. When selling to a Director, make sure it is fun for them. Your product or service has to enhance their life or the lives of others or they will not want to buy. Make sure your product is unique and creative. Does it help them overcome challenges, perform better, or aid them in achieving their life's purpose? If your product or service addresses these issues, you will have success with Directors.

Lori Greiner, a Relator, is the defender of the little guy. Often she will invest more in people than the actual products. Her top investment was a children's clothing line called RuffleButts for $600,000 for a nine percent stake. As a Relator, she cares about helping others be successful. When you are selling to a Relator, make sure your products or services help them and those they care about. Does it connect them to their family and friends? Does it serve the community as a whole? Will it give back to others? If your product or service addresses these issues, you will have success with Relators.

Daymond John, an Intellectual, invested $500,000 into Hells Bells Helmets for a fifty percent share. When you think of the systems necessary to protect the brain in a helmet and the approvals needed from the government and the Department of Transportation, you want an Intellectual to be the top investor. When selling to an Intellectual, make sure you have your i's dotted and t's crossed. They are thorough and well-read. Give them the time to research your product or service to make a decision. If your product or service addresses these issues, you will have success with Intellectuals.

Has anyone ever closed these same five sharks on a single deal? Yes, but not until Season 5, Episode 2. Before I show you how they did it, the strategy can be found in the Cuban Missile Crisis.

In the early 1960s, the United States and Russia were on the brink of World War III. Nuclear missiles were directed toward both fronts. It was President Kennedy against Premier Khrushchev. Then, for thirteen days, the Cuban Missile Crisis almost became explosive. Fortunately,

a CIA analyst was reviewing the photos from the U2 spy plane over Cuba. As he entered the oval office explaining to the executive branch that Russia was assisting Cuba, everyone demanded proof.

Kennedy could not afford another Bay of Pigs, the failed invasion to overthrow Castro in April 1961. It was one year later, and the stakes were high. The analyst threw down the black and white photos and said, "Look, they have soccer fields!" The generals and President looked at each other for some type of understanding as to why soccer fields mattered. The analyst exclaimed, "Cubans play baseball, Russians play soccer!" He had deduced that the fields indicated the presence of a Soviet military camp nearby.

When Russia sent twenty-five ships toward Cuba, the White House thought it was the early stages of World War III. At the last minute, Khrushchev acknowledged the presence of Soviet missiles in Cuba but argued they were merely defensive, and he promised to remove them if JFK promised not to invade Cuba.

World War III was averted by the same technique you can use to drastically increase your sales: "Pay Attention to the Obvious." Oliver Wendell Holmes said it best: "We all need an education in the obvious." This one analyst saw the obvious correlation between soccer fields and Russians. If Russia would have docked twenty-five battleships on the coast of Cuba, Kennedy would have interpreted it as an act of war. Discovering the obvious allowed the president to have preemptive discussions with Khrushchev.

Once, as I sat down with my client, the branch president of KeyBank, she asked me how to understand what motivated her employees. She did not feel comfortable asking them, but she wanted to know how to improve their working conditions. I showed her how to "Pay Attention to the Obvious." People support or defend their DRIVE by what they wear, how they decorate their cubicles, the pictures on their walls, their screen savers, the car they drive, and where they live. This is also demonstrated in what groups they gravitate toward, their social circles, who they spend their time with, what hobbies they have, their bumper stickers or personalized license plates, what they put on their blogs or social networking sites, and by what they say.

With the president watching, I went up to one of the tellers who had a little statue of the Eiffel Tower and pictures of herself from around the world. I simply asked the teller, "I love the Eiffel tower. Have you been there?"

"No," she replied as she perked up, "but I am saving up to go. I have been to Greece, Athens, Germany, New York, and Australia."

"Do you love to travel?" I inquired.

She went on about where she and her husband went on their honeymoon, how she almost took a job as a flight attendant instead of working at the bank, and that she had a dream of getting a pilot's license. As I returned to talk to the president, she was shocked that I discovered so much information about the teller in such a short time. It was obvious the teller was a Director and wanted to experience life through travel.

The bank president said, "I have worked with her for eighteen months and she never told me that she liked to travel or that she wanted to be a pilot."

I smiled and said, "You never asked."

Each person has an individual DRIVE that motivates them. From our political and religious views to the homes and cars we drive, we are influenced by our DRIVE. We are all walking billboards of what motivates us, and when we pay attention to what people are showing us, we can craft a custom marketing campaign to increase our sales.

First and foremost, what people *say* defends their DRIVE. If you just focus on that, you will increase your sales. Then you can get more technical with how they decorate their environment. Let's review some quotes from the sharks and see if you can identify their key words from their DRIVE.

## *Robert Herjavec—Director* D

"Work hard . . . have fun . . . be nice . . . play fair . . . dream big. We only get one chance at this life. If you're going to play this game, play to win."

Review: "Work **hard** . . . have **fun** . . . be **nice** . . . play fair . . . dream big. We only get **one chance at this life.** If you're going to **play this game, play** to win." He is driven to play, have fun, and experience life, which is the purpose of a Director (Lifestyle).

## *Lori Greiner—Relator* R

"I Love Making Products That Make People's Lives Easier And Better!"

This quote is on the QVC.com website. Analyze her words as it pertains to DRIVE. "**I Love** Making Products That **Make People's Lives Easier And Better!**" She is driven by making people's lives easier and better, which is the root of a Relator (Community).

### (I) *Daymond John—Intellectual*

"Align yourself with the right people, forge the right relationships, and you'll set yourself up for the long run."

Did you spot his three-step system for success? "**Align** yourself with the right people, **forge** the right relationships, and you'll **set yourself up** for the long run." He is giving you his three-step system for setting yourself up for the long run, which is the point of an Intellectual (Systems).

### (V) *Mark Cuban—Validator*

"Money is a scoreboard where you can rank how you're doing against other people."

Did you spot how Cuban judges how he is being admired? "**Money is a scoreboard** where you can **rank how you're doing against other people.**" For Cuban, the easiest way for him to know if he is being admired is to rank himself against other people. A Validator is motivated by giving or receiving Admiration.

### (E) *Kevin O'Leary—Executive*

"The best motivator in the world is money, and if that doesn't work, try more money."

Can you spot his motivator? "The **best motivator** in the world **is money,** and if that doesn't work, **try more money.**" In essence, "show me the money!" In a first-world scenario, money is the proof of success, which is the root cause of an Executive (Proof).

From the products the sharks invest in, to what they say, to how they live, you can spot how their DRIVE has been an integral influence. Can you see how easy it would be to customize a sales pitch to the individual sharks based on what motivates them?

Imagine understanding the DRIVE of your potential customers; how effective would it be to speak their buying language? Think of how it could also help your relationships with your family, friends, and coworkers.

Read the following quotes from famous individuals and see if you can guess their DRIVE.

1. "Luxury is feeling unrushed. It is designing a life that allows you to do what you want with high leverage, with many options, all while feeling unrushed."
    - Director, Relator, Intellectual, Validator, Executive

2. "In business it's about people. It's about relationships."
    - Director, Relator, Intellectual, Validator, Executive

3. "The bottom line is this: systems that integrate the best of human abilities and technology are the safest for all concerned."
    - Director, Relator, Intellectual, Validator, Executive

4. "It has been my observation that most people get ahead during the time that others waste."
    - Director, Relator, Intellectual, Validator, Executive

5. "If you don't understand the details of your business you are going to fail. We've had three big ideas that we've stuck with for eighteen years, and they're the reason we're successful:
    1. Put the customer first.
    2. Invent.
    3. And be patient."
    - Director, Relator, Intellectual, Validator, Executive

6. "Lots of people want to ride with you in the limo, but what you want is someone who will take the bus with you when the limo breaks down."
   - Director, Relator, Intellectual, Validator, Executive

7. "When people say you can't do it—that it's impossible—never lose hope. Just because they couldn't doesn't mean you can't."
   - Director, Relator, Intellectual, Validator, Executive

*Answer Key*

1. **Director** = Lifestyle—Tim Ferriss
2. **Relator** = Community—Kathy Ireland
3. **Intellectual** = Systems—Capt. Sully Sullenberger
4. **Executive** = Proof—Henry Ford
5. **Intellectual** = Systems—Jeff Bezos
6. **Relator** = Community—Oprah Winfrey
7. **Validator** = Admiration—David Copperfield

## Paying Attention to the Obvious

What is the value of "Paying Attention to the Obvious" and selling to all five DRIVEs? As you begin to see the obvious signs of people's DRIVE, you will be able to design your presentation or sales pitch to enhance your closing ratios. Just take a look at the only two businesses who ever closed five sharks.

From Season 5, Episode 2, Charles Michael Yim with Breathometer was asking for $250,000. From Season 7, Episode 5, JD Claridge and Charles Manning from xCraft were asking for $500,000. These three entrepreneurs, unbeknownst to them, used DRIVE to attract all five sharks to invest in their businesses.

What was the outcome? In the tank, the sharks usually beat down the contestants and give them a lower valuation than what they are expecting. The reverse happened here as the contestants closed using DRIVE. Breathometer was valued at $2.5 million and closed with a valuation of $3.3 million, receiving $1 million on his $250,000 ask. That's a 400% increase.

JD and Charles of xCraft used DRIVE so exquisitely by asking and answering questions based on each shark's personality that the sharks started bidding each other up to change the value of the company from $2 million to $6 million. JD and Charles went in wanting $500,000 and walked out with $1.5 million. That's a 300% increase. If these guys can increase the value of their companies by millions by accidentally getting DRIVE right, imagine what you can do when you craft your pitches deliberately.

Larry H. Miller Automotive is one of the largest national car dealerships, sprawling over six states with sixty-five locations. When Larry H. Miller was alive, he was a dominant figure in the business landscape of Utah and the western United States. His family still owns the NBA Utah JAZZ. His movie theaters dot multiple states.

When I got the call to do a training at his facility, I was honored. Nationally, car salespeople have a very high turn-over rate. As I sat in the training room to speak to dozens of sales people, I noticed something. There were inspirational quotes all over the wall. I had seen this many times in different sales offices, but there was something different this time. They were all based on one DRIVE. As you read the following quotes, see if you can spot it:

*"A winner is someone who sets their goals, commits themselves to those goals, and then pursues their goals with all the ability given them."*

*"Some of us will do our jobs well and some will not, but we will be judged by only one thing—the results."*
—Vince Lombardi

*"It is hard to fail, but it is even worse to never have tried to succeed."*
—Theodore Roosevelt

*"The biggest human temptation is to settle for too little."*
—Thomas Merton

*"Winning is not a sometime thing; it's an all the time thing."*

*"The difference between a successful person and others is not a lack of strength, not a lack of knowledge, but rather a lack of will."*

Did you guess Executive? If you did, you are correct. It is not surprising that all these quotes point to an Executive DRIVE. Larry H. Miller was an Executive. In his biography, he talks about being driven to win, solving problems, having control, and providing for his family. Years later, after his passing, that culture still permeates in his company.

As I have consulted companies around the world, I see a consistent pattern: sales trainers or recruiters tend to hire or recruit someone with their same DRIVE. Oftentimes when I am interviewing an organization, fifty percent of the salesforce has the same DRIVE as the dominant salesperson.

What about the other fifty percent? Imagine if you are not an Executive and your sales trainer is. Are you going to resonate with their sales techniques? Probably not. You are going to walk out of your training and try to sell as an "Executive" based on the training you received.

It will not resonate with you, nor with four out of five people you try to sell to. So, you don't hit your sales numbers, your manager puts pressure on you, and after a couple of months you feel it's not a good fit so you leave. This is one of the main reasons the sales industry has such a high turn-over rate.

If you are an owner, manager, or sales recruiter, the solution is to identify your sales peoples' DRIVE and then craft your sales training to meet each DRIVE. You can even ask the Directors in the room to put a presentation together to sell to other Directors. Do the same thing with the Relators, Intellectuals, Validators, and Executives.

We have all heard of the Golden Rule: "Do unto others as you would like them to do unto you." That is actually very selfish. It means I am going to treat you or sell to you based on my DRIVE and not yours. Instead, use the Platinum Rule by Dr. Tony Alessandra: "Do unto others the way they want to be done unto." In essence, treat them the way they want to be treated: based on their DRIVE.

Have you ever done everything right in the sales process and you still got a no? Let me show you how to turn a no into a yes.

# You Are the Next Contestant on . . .

$the PRICE is Right

# 6

# Reassociation: Turning a No into a Yes

## How To Turn a No into a Yes

How do you turn a no into a yes? Or better yet, how do you turn a "Hell NO!" into "Hell Yeah!"? As comedian and actor Drew Carey was walking out of Cracker Barrel to his car, his agent called and asked, "How would you like to take over for Bob Barker on *The Price Is Right*?"

©ZUMA Press, Inc. / Alamy Stock Photo

With disgust in his voice, Carey replied, "I am *not* doing that old man show. Are you kidding me?"

A couple of weeks later he was sitting in the parking lot of Bob's Big Boy and his agent called again, insistent. "CBS casting wants to meet with you." To be polite, Carey took the meeting. Throughout it, however, his mind was still in a "Hell no—I am not doing this old man show" mentality.

At the end of the meeting, the producer could read Carey's body language and knew he was not interested. In one last-ditch effort he asked, "What is your favorite thing to do?"

Pondering for a second, Carey said, "I love to give big tips."

The producer responded with, "On the *Price Is Right* you get to give big tips every day." This singular statement caused a major shift in the way Carey was feeling and defending his position.

## Association and Reassociation

An association is, quite simply, the connection we make between two things. Do you have a favorite sports team or alma mater you support? What is the best vacation you have ever taken? What is your favorite food? Those are all positive associations you have created throughout your life. Our associations are emotional connections we make in our brain to specific events. The technical definition is, "something linked in memory or imagination to a thing or person."

When you analyze why you like a certain sports team, alma mater, vacation, or food, you can usually identify a connection you may have shared with a family member, friend, or loved one. These connections form our associations. Over time, as we form our opinions and preferences, we begin to defend and support these associations as they morph into part of our identities.

Have you ever heard a song you have not heard for years, and it takes you back to a specific memory? Does your mind rush with a flood of memories you have not thought about for a long time? Most of us have had that experience. That song links previous experiences (usually emotional) to a catchy beat or lyric.

Kenny Chesney captured the process of an association in his song "I Go Back." He referenced how John Mellencamp's song "Jack and Diane" was a link to his high school days. In the lyrics, he says:

"Jack and Diane" painted a picture of my life and my dreams,
Suddenly this crazy world made more sense to me
Well I heard it today and I couldn't help but sing along
'Cause every time I hear that song

I go back to a two-toned short bed Chevy
Drivin' my first love out to the levy
Livin' life with no sense of time
And I go back to the feel of a fifty yard line
A blanket, a girl, some raspberry wine
Wishin' time would stop right in its tracks
Every time I hear that song, I go back, I go back.

We all have positive and negative associations. If I asked you, "Who is the one person who has shown you unconditional love?" Often, within seconds, your mind identifies someone. If I ask, "Who is the one person who has caused you the most pain?" Sometimes that name will pop into your mind faster than the previous one.

That is an association. You have linked love and pain respectively to different people (sometimes they can be the same person). Think of a particular brand you are loyal to, like a car, clothing, musical band, sports apparel, airline, computer, or phone company. The connections we make with brands and the loyalty we show them through our purchasing power is motivated by our associations.

When you pitch your product or services to a potential client, you are dealing with strong, long-held beliefs and preexisting emotional associations. Therefore, sometimes you feel hesitation from them. They have been cultivating and defending their associations their entire life. For you to come in and disrupt that is where you find resistance. However, there is a technique to changing someone from a no to a yes. It's called a Reassociation.

What is a Reassociation? It is consciously changing one's perspective to produce a new desired outcome.

During the 1990s, Carey was on two different prime time television shows: *The Drew Carey Show*, which ran for nine seasons (1995 to 2004), and *Whose Line Is It Anyway* (1998 to 2007). By the time he walked away from those shows, he had a net worth north of $150 million. When he got that call from his agent, he had a strong association with the notion that he was retired. There was no desire to host that "Old Man's Game Show," but when the producer asked "What do you love to do?" and Carey replied "I love to give big tips!", the producer responded with, "On the *Price Is Right* you get to give big tips every day."

The producer created a Reassociation by changing Carey's perspective on *The Prices Is Right* from being an "Old Man's Game Show" to an opportunity where he gets to fulfill his passion for "giving big tips." In essence, he tapped into Carey's DRIVE by using what I call the Conversation Close to discover what he was passionate about, and then linked *The Price Is Right* to meet his passion.

Since our associations are well established and compounded by years of supporting and defending them, you would think it would be near impossible to change them. On the contrary; it is quite easy as long as you follow the Law of Value. The Law of Value states, "You will exchange anything you have for something you value more."

Carey was a retired multi-millionaire. However, he was willing to exchange his retirement for the value exchange of changing people's lives by giving away bedroom sets, couches, campers, vacations, and cars.

When you are selling, the strategy is to create such a powerful and lasting Reassociation that your potential customers will want your product or service more than a competitor's. In the next couple of chapters, you will see how easy and systematic this is when you start presenting to customers based on their DRIVE versus yours.

Remember this line: "Behavior will not change until the Reassociation occurs." Another way to say this is, "The sale will not happen until the Reassociation occurs." Carey's behavior (being retired) would never have changed unless the producer created a Reassociation.

To fully understand how to create Reassociations for your clients, take a moment and see how they have sculpted your life. This will give you an insight into how to rebrand and market your products to complement a client's DRIVE.

### *What was your Reassociation?*

- What was your Reassociation for quitting your last job?
- What was your Reassociation to a previous relationship?
- What was your Reassociation during the last economic recession?
- If you have been divorced, what was that Reassociation?
- If you have ever lost weight or gotten healthy, what was that Reassociation?
- If you have ever started your own business, what was that Reassociation?
- If you have ever been in love, what was that Reassociation?

As you probably noticed, you have experienced both positive and negative Reassociations in your life. Business is no different. Companies, brands, and customer loyalty live and die by positive and negative reassociation.

## Negative Business Reassociations

- In 1949, being a post-war wealthy industrialist, Ferruccio celebrated his success by buying matching Ferraris for him and his wife. When customers would visit his tractor factory and sign a contract, he would take them to his favorite restaurant in the Ferrari.

  After burning out the clutch for a fourth time, he instructed his tractor mechanic to pull out the engine and clutch to see if there was a better solution. Quickly, he discovered Ferrari was using the exact same clutch that he put in his small tractors. The only difference was instead of the ten lire he was used to paying, Ferrari charged a thousand lire for the same part.

Infuriated, Ferruccio cornered Enzo Ferrari at an event and said, "You build your beautiful cars with my tractor parts!" Enzo Ferrari told him: "You are a tractor driver, you are a farmer. You shouldn't complain driving my cars because they're the best cars in the world."

Ferruccio told him, "Oh, yes, I am a farmer! I'll show you how to make a sports car by myself . . . to show you how a sports car has to be."

Ferruccio Lamborghini, Ferrari's one-time customer, became his greatest competitor because of this negative Reassociation.

- When Richard Branson was getting Virgin Records off the ground, he had an opportunity to sign a new band he was impressed with. He took the band to his favorite restaurant after working out the terms of the deal. The restaurateur, whom Branson knew, brought out a platter after the meal with ten marijuana joints on it. This was the '70s and, so as not to offend the owner, everyone accepted the gift.

  The deal was ready, just awaiting a signature. The next morning the band called Branson and told him they had decided to sign with PolyGram rather than Virgin. Ten years later, Branson learned from a book he was reading why the band had backed out. According to the book, the band did not sign because later that night when they got back to their hotel, they had a Reassociation.

  They thought Branson had tried to trick them into signing by getting them stoned. Branson calculated his friendship with the restaurateur had cost his company $500 million. The band went on to sell millions of albums and win multiple Grammys®. The band was Dire Straits.

- According to ESPN writer Ethan Sherwood Strauss, Nike lost Steph Curry with one negative Reassociation. Curry's godfather,

Greg Brink, worked for Nike. Growing up, Curry wore Nike, and sixty-eight percent of all NBA drafts signed with Nike. When Curry signed into the NBA, he followed suit and signed with the shoe giant. In his breakout fifty-four-point game at Madison Square Garden on Feb. 28, 2013, he was wearing Nike Zoom Hyperfuse.

In 2013, his contract had expired, and it was time to renew. According to *Forbes,* Nike accounted for 95.5 percent of the basketball sneaker market in 2014. Nike had every advantage when it came to keeping Curry. The August meeting took place on the second floor of the Oakland Marriott, three levels below Golden State's practice facility. Famed Nike power broker and LeBron James adviser Lynn Merritt was not present, a possible indication of the priority—or lack thereof—that Nike was placing on the meeting.

The meeting did not start well when the Nike employee accidentally addressed Stephen as "Steph-on," the moniker, of course, of Steve Urkel's alter ego on *Family Matters*. It got worse from there. A PowerPoint slide featured Kevin Durant's name instead, presumably left on by accident, possible residue from repurposed materials. Curry, not feeling validated, passed on the obvious choice of renewing with Nike to go over to Under Armour. This Reassociation has since added $14 billion in sales to Under Armour's bottom line.

## Positive Business Reassociations

©WENN Rights Ltd / Alamy Stock Photo

- Kathy Ireland is one of the richest supermodels in the world. She has graced the covers of many magazines, but her most distinguishing cover was on *Forbes* when she was dubbed a Super Mogul. Her net worth is higher than Christie Brinkley, Heidi Klum, Kate Moss, Naomi Campbell, Elle Macpherson, and Claudia Schiffer *combined.* How did Ireland so drastically separate herself from her peers? It came down to two different Reassociations.

  In 1993, at the height of her modeling career, Kathy Ireland was America's sex symbol. She appeared in *Sports Illustrated* swimsuit issues for thirteen consecutive years and adorned its cover three times. Marketer John Moretz approached Ireland with an offer most people would consider insulting. He didn't want her modeling swimsuits or a fashion line; he wanted to put her name on Gold Toe socks.

  Instead of snubbing the idea because of her celebrity ego, she had a Reassociation and counter-offered with, "What if we went into business together making and selling Kathy Ireland socks?" Moretz liked the idea. The product quickly sold out. Over the next couple of years, they expanded the product line into additional apparel products. In 1998, Ireland's mastermind group gave her a second Reassociation that would solidify her mogul status.

They said, "In apparel, every celebrity has a product line or is pitching one. But precious few celebrity licensors dabble in home furnishings, even though the dynamics of buying a dresser are no different from buying a dress." To expand, she partnered with Bush furniture and Shaw carpets. Her business does $400 million in Kathy Ireland replacement windows. Collectively, her licensed products do $2 billion a year in sales. In comparison, Martha Stewart's do $900 million in sales.

- Scientists and marketing directors at Proctor & Gamble were all thinking the same thing, though no one said it: "If we get fired, what happens exactly? Do security guards show up and walk us out, or do we get some kind of warning beforehand?" After spending years in R&D and dumping millions into ads and product development for a new cleaning product called Febreze, the team was fearing for their jobs.

  Due to the effectiveness of Febreze for erasing smells, the marketing department thought people would want to use it to remove rancid smells in their homes. But what they found out by interviewing customers was that, though their homes reeked, they did not notice their own stench. If you have ever raised teenage boys going through puberty, you know this is true. They don't realize they smell. The executives voted to cancel the product. The scientist begged for a couple more months. They reviewed thousands of hours of videos of customers cleaning and finally saw the Reassociation.

  People did not use the product at the beginning of the cleaning cycle but instead at the end as a mini celebration for a clean room. They changed the slogan from "Gets bad smells out of fabric" to "Breathe Happy." What was the value of this

Reassociation from trying to remove people's bad odors to a reward after cleaning with a crisp, fresh Febreze smell? Within two months, sales doubled. By the end of the first year, customers were snatching up the product to the tune of $230 million. Febreze currently does over a billion dollars annually.

- As rap legend Dr. Dre walked out on his deck at his Malibu mansion, he saw record producer Jimmy Iovine walking on the beach and hollered to him to come over. "My attorney is pitching me to do sneakers," said Dre. "F*** sneakers, do speakers!" exclaimed Jimmy.

  By the next Monday, Iovine called Dre into his conference room and had 100 samples of headphones laid out for him to review. From that one Reassociation they formed the headphone company Beats by Dre. Their most brilliant marketing campaign was during the 2012 London Olympic games. Headphone company Bose had spent millions to be the official sponsor of the games. Beats wanted to steal the spotlight from their competitor and create a Reassociation in the eyes of the public that they were fresh and cutting edge.

  To do so they rented a building down the street from the Olympic village and told athletes if they visited the store they could get a free set of Beats in their country's colors, if they took a picture with them on and posted it on social media. The Reassociation for the Olympians: take a picture, get a free set of Beats. The Reassociation for the TV viewers: If I want to perform like an Olympian I need to work out while wearing Beats. In twelve days, they collaborated with 4000 athletes and got two billion media impressions, all for

Beats: Koray Akar / Shutterstock.com

only the cost of the headphones. The marketing Reassociation worked, and sales skyrocketed. Two years later, on August 1st, 2014, Apple purchased Beats for $3 billion.

## All Marketing Is a Reassociation

In 1999, *AdAge* declared De Beers' "A Diamond is Forever" as the most memorable slogan of the twentieth century. The Reassociation is if you want your marriage to last forever, then you should show your fiancée that you are willing to cement that promise with a diamond. De Beers also worked with Hollywood and the Marilyn Monroe song "Diamonds Are A Girl's Best Friend." So, if I am proposing to my girlfriend, marketing has taught me two Reassociations: "Diamonds are Forever" and "Diamonds are a girl's best friend." I am then willing to spend a minimum of two month's salary (also a De Beers ad) to buy her the ring.

Think back to the 1980s when three elderly ladies in front of the camera said, "Where's the beef!?" This ad for Wendy's skyrocketed sales. Wendy's uses square patties, and when those square edges stretch past the round bun, you see "the beef." The Reassociation was quick and obvious; Wendy's has the beef and other fast-food chains don't. The ad was credited with boosting Wendy's annual revenue by a whopping thirty-one percent.

In the late '70s, Reebok was the predominant shoemaker. Nike wanted in the game. Their "Just Do It" ad became the Reassociation to not have any excuses. If you wanted to run a marathon, "Just Do It." If you wanted to lose those ten pounds, "Just Do It." If you want to win, "Just Do It." This Reassociation kicked off the fitness craze of the '80s and has given them supremacy in the shoe industry ever since.

The best company slogans or taglines create a Reassociation:

1. "There are some things money can't buy. For everything else, there's MasterCard"
2. "Melts in Your Mouth, Not in Your Hands" (M&M's)
3. "A Diamond Is Forever" (De Beers)
4. "Think Different" (Apple)
5. "Because You're Worth It" (L'Oréal Paris)
6. "Got Milk?" (California Milk Processor Board)
7. "Designed for Driving Pleasure" (BMW)
8. "The Quicker Picker Upper" (Bounty)
9. "Like a Good Neighbor, State Farm is There"
10. "Maybe she's born with it. Maybe it's Maybelline"

The purpose of a Reassociation is to influence action. Does your marketing message create a Reassociation? Are people drawn to take action? The sale will not happen until the Reassociation occurs.

As I interviewed Ron Klein, a vivacious and energetic seventy-eight-year-old man who has accomplished extraordinary things, it became very clear he was a problem solver. His innovative ideas have changed the world. He is the inventor of the magnetic strip on the credit card and is the developer of computerized systems for real estate multiple listing services (MLS).

As we talked, I discovered his DRIVE was an Executive. While discussing his industry-changing inventions he said, "I don't sell ideas. I sell benefits." When you are selling based on DRIVE, you have to match the right benefits to the right DRIVE to make a win-win scenario. Each of the five personalities buys based on how a product's benefits match their personal DRIVE.

In 2011, there were more active cell phones in the United States than people living there. With over 324 million activated phones it was by far one of the most common products in every household. Other than the fact you needed one in modern society, when looking at your DRIVE, what cell phone benefits appeal to you? Here are some basic benefits that appeal to Directors, Relators, Intellectuals, Validators, and Executives.

### Director

- Can be free and independent doing business anywhere
- Can customize their cover and screen saver
- Flexibility and mobility

### Relator

- Can be connected anytime to friends and family
- Can keep track of their kids
- Apps to connect to their community

### Intellectual

- Efficient
- Able to use apps to organize their life
- Able to read and learn anytime anywhere

### Validator

- The dual cameras take better pictures
- Social media apps to post their lifestyle
- Has to have the newest and best one

### Executive

- Wants the top of the line
- Can work anywhere and get things done
- Apps that will help them reach their goals

When you are selling, match the benefits of your product to the challenges a Director, Relator, Intellectual, Validator, or Executive faces.

**Director:** They are motivated by creating their ideal lifestyle. The problem you solve is helping them enhance their lifestyle with your products, services, or message.

**Relator:** They are motivated by Community. The problem you solve is helping them strengthen their community with your products, services, or message.

**Intellectual:** They are motivated by Systems. The problem you solve is by helping them find the rights system to use with your products, services, or message.

**Validator:** They are motivated by Admiration. The problem you solve is by helping them give and receive more admiration with your products, services, or message.

**Executive:** They are motivated by Proof. The problem you solve is by helping them achieve their goals and objectives with your products, services, or message.

Take five to ten minutes and list all the benefits of your product or service. Then match them to each individual DRIVE. This will help you know how to match your benefits to your customer's DRIVE.

Director:

- ______________________________
- ______________________________
- ______________________________

Relator:

- ______________________________
- ______________________________
- ______________________________

Intellectual:

- ______________________________
- ______________________________
- ______________________________

Validator:

- ______________________________
- ______________________________
- ______________________________

Executive:

- ______________________________
- ______________________________
- ______________________________

Imagine being able to spot and identify anyone's DRIVE. How quickly would you be able to increase your sales? I want to introduce you to a client of mine who created a system to spot his potential client's DRIVE. In his first twenty-four hours of using this system, he closed $50,000 in sales. Here is how you can, too.

## How To Section

- How To Discover Someone's DRIVE
- How To Create Niches To Riches
- How To Close The Sale With ASK. Don't Tell.
- How To Close The Sale With SHOW. Don't Tell.
- How To Save The Sale With P.I.C.K.S.
- Bonus Case Studies:
  - DRIVE Sales Through Borrowing An Audience
  - Decorating With DRIVE To Increase Sales
  - DRIVE In Pop Culture (Movies and TV)

FEDERAL RESERVE NOTE
HF 53349619 E
F6
100
HF 53349619 E
ONE HUNDRED DOLLARS

7

# How To Discover Someone's DRIVE

I just made $50,000 in 24 hr. using DRIVE. Do you want me to show you how I did it?"

This was the text that would change my world forever, and hopefully yours as well. It came from my client Mitch Nelson who was Rookie of the Year in his sales company and was one of the top overall income earners. With a text like that, I called him immediately and scheduled a meeting.

What he did was pure genius. I had developed DRIVE as part of another book to help people identify what motivates them. He flipped it to see what DRIVEs other people during the sales process, and in so doing closed $50,000 in sales in one day. He took the seven words for each DRIVE (see chapter 1) and put them on 3x5 cards. Then he laid them in front of his potential clients and said, in essence, "I want to get to know you better, and I have this simple DRIVE personality profile that will help me to help you. Put these cards in order based on what makes you *feel* important, not what is important to you." As each potential client read the cards and then put them in the proper order, Nelson could instantly customize his pitch to their buying language.

Seeing the power of what this could mean for salespeople and sales organizations, I decided to create a professional DRIVE card system that anyone anywhere could use to know the buying motivators of a potential client in under five minutes. Another benefit with the cards is that on the back I included a cheat sheet for each personality on how they prefer to be sold and the best locations to close them.

It was my greatest desire to include them in this book, but it was near impossible from a manufacturing standpoint. Instead, you can get your own set for fifty percent off using the code DRIVEBOOK at www.DriveSalesBook.com.

"I know what you are doing, but it doesn't feel like you are selling me; it feels like a conversation." Alex Glaittli, from Chapter 1, had spent ten months trying to sell his best friend without success. When he put the DRIVE Sales Cards down in front of his friend and asked him to put them in the order of what made him *feel* important, he knew what he valued and then could serve him without being salesy.

Too often people have commission breath. No one likes to be sold, but people love to buy. When you are sharing your product or service based on DRIVE, they feel like they are buying—not being sold.

*Here are the different ways to discover someone's DRIVE:*

1. The DRIVE Cards—see DRIVESalesBook.com/cards
2. The DRIVE Handout—see DRIVESalesBook.com/handout
3. DiscoverYourDRIVE.com—a website to understand your DRIVE
4. Have them take the assessment from Chapter 1
5. Conversation Close: The three questions listed below

## DRIVE Card/Handout Script

While sitting in a studio recording three separate Masterclasses for DRIVE, the executive producer asked me if he could try to sell me based on my DRIVE. Intrigued by the idea of experiencing DRIVE from a consumer's perspective, the thought excited me. I handed him my DRIVE Cards and said, "Give it your best shot."

He laid out the cards and after identifying my primary and secondary DRIVE, he closed the living daylights out of me. I was utterly shocked. I could not believe that even though I knew what he was doing my subconscious buying triggers were lighting up as he tied his product to my Director/Relator DRIVE. I just started laughing and said, "I want you doing this on camera." I literally had him for an hour and a half selling miscellaneous products to the different DRIVEs of business owners who were in the studio. It was brilliant because it confirmed to me that anyone could learn DRIVE and in a very short time be a proficient and professional salesperson.

Having been in sales for decades, I have always resisted scripts, and to be transparent, I still do. The following scripts are only recommendations to help you understand the information you are trying to convey so you can create the presentation in your own natural voice.

As you go through this process, note that the most crucial part is that the client identifies *their* DRIVE based on what makes them *FEEL important*, NOT what *IS important* to them. There is a huge distinction between the two. Family or work can *be* important to you, but they may not make you *feel* important. You want to connect with them on an emotional, passionate level by identifying what makes them feel important, what makes them feel on top of the world, and what connects them to their true identity.

### *Generic Script:*

- "I have come across something that has really helped me understand what DRIVEs me. I would love to know what DRIVEs you. I have this simple DRIVE personality assessment." (Start laying down the cards.) "Read each of these cards, then read them again while ranking them based on the card with the most words that ***make you feel important,*** not what is important to you. For example, work and family may be important to you, but work and family may not make you ***feel*** important. Which card has the most words that makes you ***feel*** important?"

**Pre-set Agenda Appointment**—This is when you and your customers have a pre-set agenda. For example, if you were a financial planner and you had set an appointment, they already know you are there to talk to them about diversifying their portfolio. I would say:

- "What is the #1 reason why you want to diversify your portfolio?" (Listen to their response as it will be connected to their DRIVE.) Then say, "To better serve you, I have discovered an amazing personality profile that will help me identify what DRIVEs you to make sure I recommend the right products to best serve your needs."

  (Start laying down the cards) "Read each of these cards, then read them again while ranking them based on the card with the most words that ***make you feel important,*** not what is important to you. For example, work and family may be important to you, but work and family may not make you ***feel*** important. Which card has the most words that makes you ***feel*** important?"

**Follow Up Appointment**—In this scenario you have already introduced the product, you have built a relationship of trust, and now you are doing the follow-up.

- "When we talked last you mentioned your needs were . . ." (Address their previous concerns.) "To make sure we have the right product/service to satisfy your needs, I would like to know what really DRIVEs you. I have come across a powerful personality profile that has helped me in my relationships and business. It will better help me to serve you."

  (Start laying down the cards.) "Read each of these cards, read them again while ranking them based on the card with the most words that ***make you feel important,*** not what is important to you. For example, work and family may be important to you, but work and family may not make you ***feel*** important. Which card has the most words that makes you ***feel*** important?"

With their primary and secondary DRIVE (the top two they chose) in front of you, confirm it by saying, "Based on DRIVE, you are a (say their primary and secondary). They tend to be motivated by (match it to the DRIVE motivation). Does that resonate with you?" This is the first buy-in. Then tell them your primary/secondary. "I am motivated by (match it to the DRIVE motivation)." This opens up transparency between you.

D. Director = Lifestyle
R. Relator = Community
I. Intellectual = Systems
V. Validator = Admired
E. Executive = Proof

For example, if I had just finished going through DRIVE with someone, I would say, "Based on DRIVE, you are an Executive/Intellectual. They tend to be motivated by Proof and Systems. Does that resonate with you? I am a Director/Relator. I am motivated by *Lifestyle* and *Community*."

With their primary and secondary identified, you can now ask a follow-up question 100 percent tailored to them. I have included a script specific to each of the primary and secondary combinations.

## D Director Buying Motivators (Primary)

- Experiencing Life
- Life's Purpose
- Freedom
- Creativity
- Performing
- Overcoming
- Appearance

DIRECTOR - Relator:
"If I could show you a way to achieve your life's purpose, and feel free and independent as you live the lifestyle you want while supporting your most important and valued relationships through (insert your product or service), would that be worth fifteen minutes of your time?"

DIRECTOR - Intellectual:
"If I could show you a way to achieve your life's purpose, and feel free and independent as you live the lifestyle you want by accessing a proven step-by-step system to succeed through (insert your product or service), would that be worth fifteen minutes of your time?"

DIRECTOR - Validator:
If I could show you a way to achieve your life's purpose, and feel free and independent as you live the lifestyle you want while continuing to be an example to people who want to follow through (insert your product or service), would that be worth fifteen minutes of your time?"

DIRECTOR - Executive:
If I could show you a way to achieve your life's purpose, and feel free and independent as you live the lifestyle you want while achieving your goals and providing at a higher level through (insert your product or service), would that be worth fifteen minutes of your time?"

## *Relator Buying Motivators (Primary)* R

- Relationships
- Influence
- Service
- Family
- Friends
- Parent
- Spirituality

RELATOR - Director:
"If I could show you a way to support your most important and valued relationships and engage with a community of fun, spontaneous people while experiencing life the way you want through (insert your product or service), would that be worth fifteen minutes of your time?"

RELATOR - Intellectual:
"If I could show you a way to support your most important and valued relationships and engage with a community of intelligent people who are using a proven, step-by-step system to succeed through (insert your product or service), would that be worth fifteen minutes of your time?"

RELATOR - Validator:
"If I could show you a way to support your most important and valued relationships and engage with a service-minded community while continuing to be an example people want to follow through (insert your product or service), would that be worth fifteen minutes of your time?"

RELATOR - Executive:
"If I could show you a way to support your most important and valued relationships while achieving your goals, solving problems, and providing at a higher level through (insert your product or service), would that be worth fifteen minutes of your time?"

## I Intellectual Buying Motivators (Primary)

- Knowledge
- Learning
- Health
- Nature
- Moment
- Standards
- Organized

INTELLECTUAL - Director:
"If I could help you access a proven step-by-step system that would give you the knowledge you need to succeed while achieving your life's purpose and living the lifestyle you want through (insert your product or service), would that be worth fifteen minutes of your time?"

INTELLECTUAL - Relator:
"If I could help you access a proven step-by-step system that would give you the knowledge you need to succeed while supporting your most important and valued relationships through (insert your product or service), would that be worth fifteen minutes of your time?"

INTELLECTUAL - Validator:
"If I could help you access a proven step-by-step system that would give you the knowledge you need to succeed while continuing to be an example people who want to follow through (insert your product or service), would that be worth fifteen minutes of your time?"

INTELLECTUAL - Executive:
"If I could help you access a proven step-by-step system that would give you the knowledge you need to succeed while achieving your goals and providing at a higher level through (insert your product or service), would that be worth fifteen minutes of your time?"

## *Validator Buying Motivators (Primary)* (V)

- Recognition
- Accepted
- Praise
- Trust
- Respect
- Validation
- Being Needed

VALIDATOR - Director:
"If I could show you how to recognize your strengths, trust your ability to make a difference, and be an example people want to follow while achieving your life's purpose and living the lifestyle you wish to through (insert your product or service) would that be worth fifteen minutes of your time?"

VALIDATOR - Relator:
"If I could show you how to recognize your strengths, trust your ability to make a difference, and be an example people want to follow while supporting your most important and valued relationships through (insert your product or service), would that be worth fifteen minutes of your time?"

VALIDATOR - Intellectual:
"If I could show you how to recognize your strengths, trust your ability to make a difference, and be an example, people want to follow, while using a proven step-by-step system to succeed through (insert your product or service) would that be worth fifteen minutes of your time?"

VALIDATOR - Executive:
"If I could show you how to recognize your strengths, trust your ability to make a difference, and be an example people want to follow while

achieving your goals and providing at a higher level through (insert your product or service), would that be worth fifteen minutes of your time?"

## E *Executive Buying Motivators (Primary)*

- Winning
- Control
- Work
- Goals
- Security
- Providing
- Problem Solving

EXECUTIVE - Director:
"If I could show you how to achieve your goals, solve problems, and provide for others at a higher level while attaining your life's purpose and living the lifestyle you want through (Insert our product or service), would that be worth fifteen minutes of your time?"

EXECUTIVE - Relator:
"If I could show you how to achieve your goals, solve problems, and provide for others at a higher level while supporting your most important and valued relationships through (insert your product or service), would that be worth fifteen minutes of your time?"

EXECUTIVE - Intellectual:
"If I could show you how to achieve your goals, solve problems, and provide for others at a higher level while using a proven step-by-step system to succeed through (insert your product or service), would that be worth fifteen minutes of your time?"

EXECUTIVE - Validator:
"If I could show you how to achieve your goals, solve problems, and provide for others at a higher level while continuing to be an example

people want to follow through (insert your product or service), would that be worth fifteen minutes of your time?"

Now that they are fully engaged based on their DRIVE, craft your presentation accordingly to their primary/secondary DRIVE to create a Reassociation.

Sometimes, based on the circumstance, you are not able to present the cards or the handout. During those times, use what I call the Conversation Close.

## The Conversation Close

Keith Cardinal was working as a supply-chain consultant for billion-dollar companies from SpaceX and Microsoft to Google. Being in his late fifties, he wanted to transition out of his job and go into business consulting. Within his first month, starting from zero, he applied the Conversation Close and was able to generate $25,000 in sales commission.

There will be times when you first meet someone or you are doing a phone call where it would not be ideal for laying down cards or giving them a handout. For those situations, here are three questions that will help you identify their DRIVE.

1. Other than work and family, what are you most passionate about?
2. When you don't get to (insert Passion), how does it impact you?
3. When you get to (insert Passion), how does it make you feel?

Depending on how they answer these questions, you can get a pretty good idea of their primary and secondary DRIVE. For example, if they answer that they love to travel, be creative, experience life, overcome challenges, and feel free and independent, then they are a Director. If they talk about spending time with their family, friends, and giving back to their community or church, they are a Relator. If their answer is organizing, exercising, eating healthy, being in nature, reading, or learning, then they are an Intellectual.

If their reply is doing activities where they are being validated, respected, praised, trusted, or recognized, then they are a Validator. And lastly, if their reply has to do with winning, being in control, providing, working, achieving goals, or solving problems, then they are an Executive.

The following are examples of actual clients based on the Conversation Close. See if you can identify their DRIVE from these three simple questions. The answers will be revealed at the end. Here is a quick reminder of what motivates each DRIVE.

D. Director = Lifestyle
R. Relator = Community
I. Intellectual = Systems
V. Validator = Admired
E. Executive = Proof

*Leesa Price—*

*CEO of Warrior Princess*

Question: Other than work and family, what are you most passionate about?

Answer: *I am most passionate about empowering other people, especially women.*

Question: When you don't get to "empower women," how does it impact you?

Answer: *I don't feel important, I don't feel whole, I feel like I have lost purpose and meaning.*

Question: When you are "empowering women" how does that make you feel?

Answer: *I feel incredibly blessed to have a positive impact in the lives of others.*

*Richard Stock—*

*Real Estate Investor*

Question: Other than work and family, what are you most passionate about?

Answer: *Traveling.*

Question: When you don't get to "travel," how does it impact you?

Answer: *I feel like I am failing, not being able to accomplish all that I want. Letting others down.*

Question: When you can "travel" how does that make you feel?

Answer: *I love to experience new things and cultures. I feel free and accomplished.*

*Eric Counts—*

*Professional Speaker and Credit Repair Specialist*

Question: Other than work and family, what are you most passionate about?

Answer: *Work.* (If they answer "work" or "family" let them go with their answer, it is how they get their DRIVE met)

Question: When you don't get to "work," how does it impact you?

Answer: *Very negatively, letting a lot of people down. I feel I have disappointed people.*

Question: When you get to "work" how do you feel?

Answer: *What I do gives me the validation. I feel recognized and trusted by my audience.*

*Justin Prince—*

*Co-owner of a $300 million sales company*

Question: Other than work and family, what are you most passionate about?

Answer: *I feel called to serve and inspire people.*

Question: When you don't get to "inspire and serve people," how does it impact you?

Answer: *I feel terrible. I feel like a slothful servant, out of alignment, disenchanted.*

Question: When you get to "inspire and serve people" how do you feel?

Answer: *It makes me feel like what I was put on earth to do. Completely full, purposeful, what I do matters.*

*Christian George—*

*Educational Development—Entrepreneur/Investor*

Question: Other than work and family, what are you most passionate about?

Answer: *Learning, knowledge, creating systems, contributing.*

Question: When you don't get to "learn something new," how does it impact you?

Answer: *For me, it stifles me, it is a double whammy, I don't feel efficient and I didn't achieve what I wanted to do.*

Question: When you get to "learn something new" how do you feel?

Answer: *It's energy. If I learn a new strategy, I have more time in the day and can get more done.*

### *Daniela Camacho—*
### *Corporate Manager*

Question: Other than work and family, what are you most passionate about?

Answer: *Working and putting money in the bank.*

Question: When you don't get to "work and save money," how does it impact you?

Answer: *I feel stressed out and incompetent.*

Question: When you get to "work and save money" how do you feel?

Answer: *I feel at peace and safe.*

### *Answers*

1. Leesa Price—Relator
2. Richard Stock—Director
3. Eric Counts—Validator
4. Justin Prince—Relator
5. Christian George—Intellectual
6. Daniela Camacho—Executive

When using the Conversation Close, if you have not been able to clarify their DRIVE, simply tie their answers to the benefits of your product or service. Connect to their passion and you will connect to their DRIVE. For example, if you were selling to Leesa and could not identify her DRIVE, you could still tie your product or service to her empowering women. If you were selling to Richard, how would your product or service allow him to travel more? If you were selling to Eric, how would your product or service help him be validated in his profession? Be creative; you can find a link between what you do and the answers people give. If you do this alone, you will increase your sales. As you have the second or third visit with them, use the DRIVE Cards or DRIVE Handout to be more precise on what motivates them.

With the Conversation Close, you will most likely not be able to identify their secondary DRIVE. Whenever you have the chance, I always recommend using the DRIVE Cards/Handout, but for those instances when you cannot, the next most effective way to identify what makes them feel important is the Conversation Close. Like the sample scripts listed above where you ask a follow-up question based on their primary and secondary, the script below is designed for only the primary. Once again, always customize it for more authenticity. Change the wording to match your industry.

**Director:** "If I could show you a way to achieve your life's purpose, and feel free and independent as you live the lifestyle you want through (insert your product or service) would that be worth fifteen minutes of your time?"

> Example: Financial Planner selling to a Director: "If I could show you a way to achieve your life's purpose, feel free and independent as you live the lifestyle you want, through investing in a 401K or the stock market would that be worth fifteen minutes of your time?"

**Relator:** "If I could show you a way to support your most important and valued relationships and engage with a community of (insert your product or service) who are extremely focused on having a family mindset, would that be worth fifteen minutes of your time?"

> Example: Selling a business opportunity to a Relator: "If I could show you a way to support your most important and valued relationships and engage with a community of entrepreneurs who are extremely focused on having a family mindset, would that be worth fifteen minutes of your time?"

**Intellectual:** "If I could help you access a proven system that would give you the knowledge you need to succeed in (insert your product or service), as well as step-by-step instructions on how to move forward, would that be worth fifteen minutes of your time?"

Example: Selling a SAS or a CRM solution to an Intellectual: "If I could help you access a proven system that would give you the knowledge you need to succeed in working with your clients, as well as step-by-step instructions on how to move forward, would that be worth fifteen minutes of your time?"

**Validator:** "If I could show you how to recognize your strengths, trust your ability to make a difference, and continue to be an example people want to follow through (insert your product or service), would that be worth fifteen minutes of your time?"

Example: Car salesmen selling to a Validator: "If I could show you how to recognize your strengths, trust your ability to make a difference, and continue to be an example people want to follow through upgrading your car, would that be worth fifteen minutes of your time?"

**Executive:** "If I could show you how to achieve your goals, solve problems and provide at a higher level through (insert your product or service), would that be worth fifteen minutes of your time?"

Example: Real estate agent selling to an Executive: "If I could show you how to achieve your goals, solve problems, and provide at a higher level through investing in real estate, would that be worth fifteen minutes of your time?"

Now that you know their DRIVE, you can customize your presentation to meet their needs. This goes back to the 20/80 Rule. We lose eighty percent of our sales because we are selling based on our DRIVE and not our customer's. As you learn your customer's DRIVE, you have the potential to increase your sales by 400 percent.

You are compensated in direct proportion to the problems you solve. During Michael Jordan's fifteen-year professional basketball career he played in 1078 games, scored 32,292 points, was rookie of the year, 14x All Star, 11x All-NBA, 9x All-Defensive, 6x Finals MVP, and earned six champion rings. With all of his accomplishments and his life-long commitment to better himself and the game, he only made $90 million. Yes, only $90 million. Why would I say "only"? Because in 2019 he earned $134 million from Nike for his Jordan AIR brand.

Nike repeatedly pays Jordan over a hundred million dollars every year. Nike's sales for their entire shoe and apparel empire are about $30 billion, of which Jordan's line makes up ten percent at $3.2 billion. Jordan has solved more problems for Nike than he ever did for the Chicago Bulls and has been compensated accordingly.

Larry Page, co-founder of Google, said, "It is easy to be a billionaire: solve a ten billion-dollar problem." In the next section you will learn how to solve specific problems based on DRIVE to be able to increase your compensation.

8

# Niches To Riches

Will you come to Australia's Gold Coast and share DRIVE with some of the top leaders in direct selling?" Rob Sperry, one of the most respected sales trainers in the industry, had just invited me to speak at an event he and Frazer Brookes were hosting. However, it was not just an invitation; it was a secret audition to see if I could create enough value for Frazer to invite me to train at his event in the UK for 2000 salespeople. The first day I delivered DRIVE, the response was so high they asked me to create another speech for the following day.

I was given only thirty minutes. The first fifteen minutes I covered the "Why vs. How" of DRIVE, and then I had a spontaneous thought: *If this is an audition, I need to close this entire room before Frazer and Rob do on the last day. These guys are the best at what they do. I have got to stand out or I am never going to the UK. I cannot sell my product—I need to sell their product.*

Quickly, I created what I call the value stack: I illustrated the value Frazer and Rob had already built for the audience. I positioned them as seven figure earners in the industry, which they are. I addressed their influence and their millions of online followers. I asked the audience for participation about what they have learned and what their take-a-ways have been from the event.

Within minutes everyone was in unison that they believed these two individuals had changed their lives, enhanced their relationships, and helped their businesses to be more profitable. Then I asked, "By a show of hands, how many of you purchased and signed up for their mastermind?" Only ten hands went up. In the first twenty-four hours of the two-day event, only ten people had purchased. Frazer and Rob were building up for a close at the end of the event, but I knew I needed to make a huge impact as quickly as I could.

Jumping off the stage, I went into the audience, climbed up on a chair, and proclaimed, "I am going to sell the living daylights out of every one of you in this room. I am not affiliated with their product, I do not receive commissions, but I want you to know how it feels to be sold based on your DRIVE." I then instructed the Directors to stand. I pitched them for only sixty seconds on how these two leader's masterminds will make them feel free and independent, allow them to be more creative in their business, and help them to overcome challenges that will help them experience the life they truly want.

As the Relators stood, I continued, "Their product will help you build your communities, connect with your most intimate and personal relationships, as well as help you give more service." With intellectuals, I said, "These two have created more systems than anyone in the industry; they have prebuilt presentations that will increase your sales, and most importantly, on the mastermind calls you will be able to learn their cutting edge, never released sales techniques." At this point someone shouted, "Will you quit talking and just take my damn credit card already?!" Everyone burst into laughter, but I was not done.

Next were the Validators: "Do you see how being associated with the two biggest leaders in the industry will help you look like a rock star to your teams? Imagine the secrets they will teach you. As you take their training back to your teams, how will that help you lift them up and be the example they want to follow?" Lastly, the Executives. "You all want proof. You know who these two leaders are. They are the best of the best. You already know that—then what are you waiting for? You are the group who should have their credit cards out first. You want to win and take control of your business, Frazer and Rob have unprecedented success. They are going to take you across the finish line."

To add a sense of urgency, I put a scarcity clause in there that if they bought within the next twenty-four hours I would personally do a one-hour free training on DRIVE. Two hours later, by the end of lunch, there were thirty new orders, a 300 percent increase from their current standing. Within twenty-four hours, 144 people invested in their mastermind, giving them a 1440 percent increase in sales.

Rob told me later that while I was closing the room, Frazer turned to him and asked, "Do you think I can convince Woody to come and train at my UK event?" I was elated.

Target selling to each individual DRIVE is called Niches to Riches. An industry leader who has maximized this technique in their marketing is nutritional company Pharmavite, which manufactures Nature Made. They've created fifteen-second ads before YouTube videos designed specifically to address each DRIVE. One ad for an

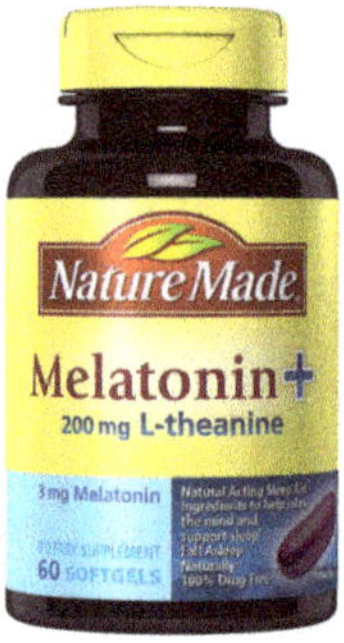


Executives says, "Individuals lose sleep each night costing them $315,000 of lost wages over their lifetime." The ad is for the sleep aid Melatonin. An Executive wants to win, and if losing sleep means they are losing performance and money, the reassociation is instant: "I need Nature Made's Melatonin." Even though Melatonin affects everyone regardless of their DRIVE, Pharmavite identified the challenges of an Executive and made a niche ad specific to this group.

Another ad directed toward Relators and Validators shows family and friends from every walk of life getting excited about a secret baby reveal. It then recommends a prenatal vitamin. All pregnant women regardless of their DRIVE would benefit from a prenatal vitamin, but the script and the images they used were targeted to Relators and Validators. For the Intellectuals, there is an ad with a pharmacist talking about the systems Nature Made has in place, the USP Dietary Supplement seal of approval, and the science behind how it is the most recommended vitamin. They are target marketing to appeal to the educated side of an Intellectual. These Niche DRIVE ads have made Nature Made one of the most recognized brands in the supplement industry with sales in 2019 of over $280 million.

Renowned watchmaker Patek Philippe (Chapter 5) was started in 1839 by two Intellectuals. Both Patek and Philippe created ads that would support their DRIVE. When the Stern family (Relators)

acquired the entire company in 1932, they switched to Relator style ads with their legacy marketing "You Never Actually Own A Patek Philippe. You Merely Look After It For The Next Generation." This is the challenge with the 20/80 Rule. Patek Philippe is a very successful company, but they are missing out on a huge market share by not addressing the remaining four buying personality types.

Here is a simple way they could market to the other DRIVEs as well as Relators. As you read these, look at your own products and services—are you accidentally alienating a certain market share?

Patek Philippe could structure ads based on the individual DRIVEs:

### *Director = Lifestyle* (D)

- Show how their watches are uniquely different than other companies and how Patek Philippe has been different since 1845.
  - There are countless wristband and watch face combinations that make the watch custom to anyone's liking.
  - Address their 80+ patents that make their watches unique from others.
  - Note the VIP experience of owning and servicing a Patek Philippe.

  These ads could target a Director's desire to enjoy a certain type of lifestyle, creativity, overcoming challenges, feeling free and independent while experiencing life on their own terms.

### *Relator = Community* (R)

- This is their current marketing strategy where they showcase how it is run by a fourth-generation Stern.
  - Family ran and operated business
  - Legacy play

These ads already address a Relator's desire to be connected to a community, family, friends, and to have a power of influence to serve and help others.

## I Intellectual = Systems

- Showcase their engineering superiority and technological advancements while still being a good global environmental citizen.
  - Address the 80+ patents and their superior hand craftsmanship.
  - In 1989, Patek Philippe created Calibre 89 for its 150th anniversary, at the time the most complicated mechanical watch ever made. The Calibre 89 holds 33 complications, including the date of Easter, time of sunrise, equation of time, and many other indicators. It's 1,728 unique parts allow sidereal time, a 2,800 star chart, and more.
  - In 2014, for its 175-year anniversary, Patek Philippe introduced the Grandmaster Chime Ref. 5175, the most complicated wristwatch ever built by the manufacturer.

Their ads could target an Intellectual's desire to create systems, be more knowledgeable, organized, healthy, and connected to nature.

## V Validator = Admiration

- Show leaders, dignitaries, celebrities, artists, and actors who have owned or used their watches.
  - Queen Elizabeth, as well as many other members of the royal family, often wear Patek Philippes (Queen Victoria even bought matching watches for herself and Prince Albert back in the nineteenth century).
  - There is a picture of Beatle John Lennon showing off his watch on his 40th birthday.

- Beatle Paul McCartney was pictured wearing one on the cover of *Rolling Stone* in 2012.
- Artist Pablo Picasso wore them and collected three watches.
- U.S. President Franklin D. Roosevelt gifted one to the Dalai Lama.
- General George Patton had one, as did Elizabeth Taylor.
- Actors wore them in TV shows and movies: Liam Neeson: *Non-Stop* (2014), Michael Douglas: *The Game* (1997), Gabriel Macht: *Suits* (2011–2017), Ryan Gosling: *Drive* (2011)

Their ads could target a Validator's desire to be admired, respected, praised, and recognized.

## *Executive = Proof* (E)

- Showcase Patek Phillipe's dominance in the watch world.
  - 1st keyless winding system 1845
  - 1st Swiss wristwatch 1868
  - 1st perpetual calendar in pocket watches 1889
  - 1st lady's wristwatch with complications 1916
  - 1st perpetual calendar in a wristwatch 1925
  - 1st all-electric clock in the world 1956
  - Still holds the record since 1962 when their tourbillion movement achieved the most precise time ever recorded.
  - The most expensive watch ever sold at auction was a Patek Philippe Grandmaster Chime Ref. 6300A-010 on November 9, 2019, fetching $31 million.

Their ads could target an Executive's desire to win, be in control, provide, and solve problems.

To make your pitches as effective as possible, market based on Niches To Riches. To craft a Niches To Riches campaign, identify how your product's benefits will solve the challenges facing each DRIVE. As you do this, you will have a home run.

To make this easier for you, I have broken down each DRIVE, their buying motivators, their challenges, recommended solutions you can provide, where to and not to close them, and what to do when selling to each one.

## How To Sell To A Director

D

Directors are motivated to create their ideal *Lifestyle.* When purchasing a product or service, they want to know how it is going to enhance their lifestyle or give them the life they want. They are attracted to products or services that will help them achieve financial freedom, time freedom, or give them a VIP experience.

Directors get frustrated when they feel trapped and are not free and independent. They get bored repeating the same thing over and over. They want to be stimulated creatively. They are bothered by other people who don't want to do something new. They get overwhelmed when they can't find a solution to their problems. They are disappointed if they are not pursuing their life's purpose.

Director's challenges:

- They feel overwhelmed.
- They do not feel free and independent.
- Their current situation doesn't make them feel creative.
- They are not pursuing their life's purpose.
- They are not performing the way they want.
- They are not experiencing life the way they want.
- They do not feel confident in their appearance.

Director's solutions: when selling to a Director make sure the benefits of your product or service helps them to:

- Be **free and independent**
- **Experience life** at a whole new level (VIP experience)
- Assist them in **overcoming obstacles**
- Work toward their **life's purpose**
- Be more **creative**
- Enhance their **appearance**
- **Perform** at a higher level

When selling to a Director:

- Does your product have a wow factor?
- Is it visually stimulating?
- Does it have an element of surprise?
- Does it make their life engaging?

Director: items that will ruin your sale:

- Boring details
- Homework
- Talking about yourself or your expertise

Director: locations where they are more inclined to buy:

- Their place/office
- Nice restaurants
- Classy lobbies
- Outdoor patio with a view

Director: locations where they are less inclined to buy:

- Classroom setting
- Boring office
- Closed in space
- Cheap restaurants
- Noisy places

Make your product's benefits address their desire to be free and independent, experiencing life, being creative, helping them achieve their life's purpose, performing at a higher level, making them confident with their appearance and/or overcoming their challenges. If you do this, you will sell to a Director.

## How To Sell To A Relator

(R)

Relators are motivated by *Community*. When purchasing a product or service, they tend to consult with family, friends, or their extended social community before making a decision. They are driven to invest in their community and are more inclined to affiliate with or purchase products that give back.

Relators are givers and often sacrifices their personal wellbeing for their community. They can be exhausted from taking care of everyone else. They are frustrated when they can't have an influence among their peers, friends, and family. They struggle when their relationships are not going well.

Relator's challenges:

- They feel insecure in their relationships.
- They don't have the influence they want.
- Exhausted from giving too much service.
- Family is not supporting them.
- Friends don't believe in them.
- They are worried for their kids.
- They are struggling to connect spiritually.

Relator's solutions: When selling to a Relator make sure the benefits of your product or service helps them to:

- Have a power of **influence**
- Enhance their **relationships**
- Strengthen their **family**
- Be better **parents** (Providing for their kids—emotionally, physically and financially)
- Deepen their relationships with their **friends**
- Provide **service** to others

- Connecting to **God, Spirit, or Universe** (spirituality as defined by them)

When selling to a Relator:

- Does your product or service help and support their community?
- Does it connect them with their loved ones?
- Will it bring them closer to other people?
- Will it make them look like a leader in their community?

Relator: items that will ruin your potential sale:

- If you ignore or do not address the people they have brought with them.
- They will often consult with friends and family before making a commitment of investment. Do not pressure them to make a decision that day.
- They are not often interested in the "nuts and bolts."

Relator: locations where they are more inclined to buy:

- Their home
- When their friends and family are present and endorse the product/service
- High attendance events, the herd mentality—social proof

Relator: location where they are less inclined to buy:

- Low attended events. They want social proof.
- Loud locations where the focus is not on them.

Make your product's benefits help them build healthy relationships with their family and friends, have a power of influence, connect to their higher power, and/or serve their community. If you do this, you will sell to a Relator.

## How To Sell To An Intellectual

I

Intellectuals are motivated by *Systems*. When purchasing a product or service, they are looking for the details, or step-by-step actions they need to take to achieve the desired goal. They want to enhance their intelligence and expertise. They desire to share what they know with others.

They get frustrated when they cannot find a system to solve their problem. They have paralysis by analysis. They will exhaust themselves by creating multiple systems to solve a task. They are bothered by others who challenge or disrupt their system.

Intellectual's challenges:

- They cannot find the information they need.
- Exhausted from reading and studying too much.
- They might not feel healthy.
- They might be too busy to connect with nature.
- Life is too stressful to be in the moment.
- They might be having their standards challenged.
- They may not feel a sense of organization.

Intellectual's solutions: When selling to an Intellectual, make sure the benefits of your product or service helps them to:

- Increase their **knowledge**
- **Learn** something new
- Honor their **standards**
- Be more **organized**
- Be in the **moment**
- Connect with **nature**
- Increase their **health**

When selling to an Intellectual:

- Does your product or service have clear step-by-step instructions on how to implement it in their life?
- Does it save them time or money? Does it make their life easier?
- Is the learning curve short and direct?

Intellectual: items that will ruin your sale:

- Too much focus on lifestyle and money
- Don't discredit them
- Inaccurate numbers

Intellectual: locations where they are more inclined to buy:

- Seated toward front
- Experiencing product
- Have online access

Intellectual: location where they are less inclined to buy:

- Loud places
- Lavish experiences
- Places without internet

Make your product's benefits help them be in the moment, connect to nature, feel healthy, honor their standards, stimulate them intellectually, and/or be more organized. If you do this, you will sell to an Intellectual.

## How To Sell To A Validator

(V)

Validators are motivated by *Admiration.* When purchasing a product or service, they are driven by how it will make them look better to their peers, friends, or family. They enjoy focus and being an example people want to follow.

If you are selling to a Validator they prefer to not be in loud, crowded places. They feel violated when people do not trust or respect them. They struggle to make a decision if there is a chance they will look stupid. They do not like to be ignored or overlooked.

Validator's challenges:

- They don't feel recognized.
- They might not feel accepted.
- Often they don't feel praised.
- They need to feel trusted.
- They might not feel respected.
- They don't feel validated.
- They need to feel needed.

Validator's solution: When selling to a Validator, make sure the benefits of your product or service helps them to:

- Give or receive **trust**
- Give or receive **praise**
- Give or receive **respect**
- Give or receive **recognition**
- Give or receive **acceptance**
- Give or receive **validation**

When selling to a Validator:

- Does your product or service make your client look like a rock star?

- Will it bring them positive attention from people?
- Does it help them look good in front of others?

Validator: items that will ruin your sale:

- Being alone
- Being disrespected
- Being ignored
- Feeling ignorant

Validator: locations where they are more inclined to buy:

- With friends
- Social settings
- In their home

Validator: location where they are less inclined to buy:

- Peer pressure
- Loud places
- Distracting places

Make your product's benefits help them be a giver or receiver of validation, praise, respect, acceptance, trust, recognition, and/or admiration. If you do this, you will sell to a Validator.

## How To Sell To An Executive

E

Executives are motivated by *Proof.* When purchasing a product or service, they want *Proof* that it works and that it is going to make their life or business better. They respond to third-party testimonials and reviews. Executives focus on the big picture of getting what they want—not the details on how to achieve it.

If you are selling to an Executive, they are frustrated if they are not winning and in control. They are exhausted from their enormous "To Do" list. They dislike people who waste their time and talk about nothing. They are constantly pushing to achieve a desired goal and are frustrated when not accomplishing a task.

Executive's challenges:

- They do not feel in control.
- They are worried about making money and providing.
- Exhausted from work.
- Feel insecure in work and family.
- They feel like there are too many problems to solve.
- Feel overwhelmed from too many goals.
- They might not feel like they are winning in their life.

Executive solution's: When selling to an Executive, make sure the benefits of your product or service helps them to:

- Feel like they are **winning**
- Have a sense of **control**
- Have success in their **work**
- Reach their **goals**
- Feel a sense of **security**
- **Provide** for the people they choose
- **Solve problems**

When Selling To An Executive:

- Does your product or service give your client more control?
- Does it help them win?
- Does it make their goals easier to achieve?

Executive: Items that will ruin your sale:

- Details
- Step-by-step instructions
- Feeling second place

Executive: Locations where they are more inclined to buy:

- Professional locations
- 5-Star restaurants
- Nice hotel lobbies

Executive: Location where they are less inclined to buy:

- Dingy places
- Crowded places
- Unprofessional places

Make your product's benefits help them feel like they are winning, have a sense of control, solve problems, achieve their goals, enhance their work productivity, and/or have more security. If you do this, you will sell to an Executive.

## Advertising with DRIVE

The mansion was full of twenty-five over-the-top business achievers who were the best in what they did. We had been sponsoring these high-level networking events every month, where we would rent exquisite properties, bring in world-renowned guest speakers, and spend one to two days networking and building each other's businesses.

This was where I first met AJ Wilcox, a ginger-haired triathlete who owns one of the largest LinkedIn ad agencies. His company, B2Linked, consults for 400+ LinkedIn Ads accounts, including half of LinkedIn's top ten accounts. While sitting around the outdoor campfire in the majestic Wasatch mountains, he turned to me and asked, "Do you think we could target market ads specific to DRIVE?"

With assuredly, I said, "Absolutely!"

He went quiet for a while, turning the coals over with a stick. "If you can do that, I think I could revolutionize my client's businesses," he said.

The next thing I knew, I was invited to his office to train his employees on how to write ads based on DRIVE.

One of the first results came from Bitbean, whose clients include Walmart, United Airlines, and CVS Pharmacy. They build custom software for "ambitious companies striving to be industry leaders." Their first ads (below) were not generating the leads they wanted to.

Version #1: "Custom software can make or break business. For some businesses, the right custom software can mean up to 5X more revenue. In this free eBook, you'll get the info you need to make the right decision about custom software."

Version #2: "Looking into getting custom software for your business but don't know where to start? In the free eBook, you'll learn everything you need to know before diving in."

Jacob Haynie, one of B2Linked Paid Media Specialists, said, "The test was targeting business owners in start-up tech companies. We believed these individuals would fit within Executive and Director DRIVE personas. Because of this, we began to run ads with copy targeting each of these personas." After identifying the DRIVE they were targeting, they then used keywords to trigger engagement and the results were astounding.

DRIVE Version #1: "**Innovation** in custom software means **more money for your business.** Find out what custom software trends **will dominate** 2020 and how **your business** can **take advantage of them to reach your goals.**"

DRIVE Version #2: "**Is your company secure** in these crazy times? Learn the **8 custom software trends** to watch out for in 2020 and how they can help your **business take control** and **overcome any problems.**"

Results:

1. The overall volume of clicks coming in jumped by 249 percent!
2. Average engagement saw a 27 percent (from 0.48 percent to 0.61 percent). Most importantly, the client saw 2.64 times more leads come in during the same time period.
3. Even better than that was that the leads coming in were 51.41 percent cheaper (average cost per lead dropped to $178.88 from $347.92). The ads also helped improve the conversion rate by 63.16 percent (from 4.18 percent to 6.82 percent).

"I'm super happy with these results!" said Jacob. "Across the board, the DRIVE ads helped improved performance. Most importantly, they helped our client generate more leads at a much lower cost per lead than any of our previous tests."

The following ads are to illustrate how to target market using keywords based on each individual DRIVE. The ads are focused on hiring sales professionals.

### (D) *Director keywords:*

- Appearance
- Overcome
- Free and Independent

- Creative
- Life's Purpose
- Performing
- Experiencing Life

Do you want to be ***free*** and ***independent***? Are you tired of not ***experiencing life*** to the fullest? Are you ready to be ***creative*** and ***overcome challenges***? If you are, "click here." I am looking for sales professionals who are ready to make a ***difference in the world.***

### Relator keywords: (R)

- Relationships
- Influence
- Service
- Family
- Friends
- Parenting
- Spirituality

Do you want to spend more time with your ***family*** and ***friends***? Is your job holding you back from helping your ***community***? If so, I am looking for sales professionals who are ***service*** minded and want to have a power of ***influence***. "Click Here" to learn how you can use your talents to positively impact others.

### Intellectual keywords: (I)

- Knowledge
- Learning
- Health
- Nature
- Moment
- Standards
- Organization

Are you looking for the ***system*** to succeed? Are you able to ***learn*** new information and put it in an ***organized*** manner to get results? If so, "Click Here." You deserve to ***know*** the 3½ steps to being a top sales professional.

### (V) *Validator keywords:*

- Recognition
- Accepted
- Praise
- Trust
- Respect
- Validation
- Being Needed

Do you feel underpaid for what you do? Do you want ***respect, praise,*** and ***validation*** for all your hard work? It's time to ***trust*** yourself and create the life you were born to have as a sales professional. "Click Here" to know how to be the leader you deserve to be.

### (E) *Executive keywords:*

- Control
- Provide
- Work
- Security
- Solving Problems
- Goals
- Winning

Are you tired of not reaching your ***goals*** and making less than you are worth? Are you ready to take ***win*** in this game called life? If you are a self-starter who can ***solve problems,*** has a good ***work*** ethic, and wants to ***provide*** their own ***security,*** then "Click Here." I am looking for sales professionals who want to take ***control*** of their own life and future.

Though it is important to niche based on each DRIVE, there are times when you want to cast a larger net. Some DRIVE personalities are attracted to similar words and phrases. If we look at the Shark Tank, you will notice Robert Herjavec and Kevin O'Leary have done the most deals together (fifteen). Robert is a Director and Kevin is an Executive. Likewise, Lori Greiner and Mark Cuban have done the most deals together (eleven). Lori is a Relator and Mark is a Validator. And Daymond John has done the least amount of deals with anyone (seven). As an Intellectual they want to create their own system.

*Sample ads for recruiting sales professionals:*

**Director-Executive**

Do you feel you are ***underpaid*** for what you do? Are you ready to take ***control*** of your own ***independence***? Are you the type who wants to ***experience life*** to the fullest, can set ***goals, overcome challenges*** and ***win***? Then "Click Here." I want to talk to you about how a career in sales can ***change your world*** forever.

**Relator-Validator**

Do you feel ***undervalued*** for all you do? Do you want to be ***recognized*** for helping your ***friends*** and ***family*** overcome their challenges? Do you want to have a ***community*** of professionals who will ***respect*** and ***praise*** you for your ***contribution***? If so, "Click Here" and let me show you how a career in sales can help ***you*** and the ***ones you care about.***

Remember, the sale does not happen until the reassociation occurs. The reassociation happens the instant you have matched the benefits from your products or services to meet your customer's DRIVE. This creates what I call a Buying Bridge.

Let me introduce you to the highest closing profession that has nearly a 100 percent closing ratio. They construct the ultimate Buying Bridge.

# 9

# ASK. Don't Tell

## ASK. Don't Tell

"My cell phone does not work. No matter what I try, the buttons do not respond." My seventy-six-year-old mother needed a new phone. To say she is electronically challenged would be an understatement. Have you ever seen the cartoon of a boy going into the "School for the Gifted" and he is "pulling" on a door that says "Push"? That's my mom. I love her to death, but this has always been the case with anything electronic.

As the Apple store opened, we went straight to the cell phones. We settled in at the Genius Bar as our salesman spent the next two hours explaining the storage capabilities, the glass, battery power, CPU diagram, etc. Finally, I said, "Mom, I need to get back to work." As we walked out of the store, I asked her if she knew how to turn the phone on.

"No," she said.

"Do you know how to send a text to the family?"

Again, "No."

"Do you know how to take a picture of your grandchildren?"

Another "No."

I said, "Let's go to lunch and I will walk you through your phone."

## Listen to Learn—Don't Assume and Assault

The salesman was an Intellectual and therefore spent hours explaining the system of the phone while showcasing his expertise. He assumed what she wanted and then assaulted her with useless information. He never asked her, "How do you plan to use your phone?" Or, "What features do you use most?"

The ironic thing was the salesman is a friend of the family who lives two doors from my parents. He is well-aware of her challenges with electronics. Like most salespeople he went straight into "Tell" mode by listing all the benefits but did not "Ask" what benefits she wanted. Every product has benefits, but if you don't match your benefits to your customer's DRIVE, then you have not created the first part of the sale—which is the Reassociation.

This ties back into the 20/80 Rule. When we revert to just telling customers the benefits, we sell based on our DRIVE, not theirs, thereby potentially losing eighty percent of sales just by opening our mouths. When you ASK (A.S.K.—Always Seek Knowledge), you listen to learn how you can solve their problems with your products.

## Build A Buying Bridge

Which profession has the highest closing ratio over any other profession? It has nearly a 100 percent closing ratio. It's doctors. Why? It is simple. They ask questions. Every time you meet with a potential client, visualize two shorelines with a river running between them. You are on one side and your potential client is on the other side. The river is their fears, anxieties, preconceived ideas, associations, and opinions.

Your job is to create a Buying Bridge from your side to theirs. If you don't make this bridge, you cannot sell them. If you do not sell them, you cannot serve them. When we "tell" people the benefits of our products or services, all we do is build a wall between us and them. As you ask questions and they answer them, you begin to create a Reassociation; that process of questions and answers is what builds this bridge.

Imagine walking into a doctor's office and she starts telling you the benefits of a colonoscopy and how it helps detect colon cancer. And how one in every twenty Americans will develop colon cancer, and colonoscopies are the most effective means of prevention, diagnosis, and treatment. No other colon cancer screening is as thorough and comprehensive.

She then says, "Let's get you in today at 2:00 p.m. for your colonoscopy."

And you say, "Doctor, thank you but I am just here for a flu shot."

Without asking you any questions, all she has done is build a wall between your problem and the benefits she could have provided you. The reason doctors have such a high closing ratio is because they follow a three-part *ASK. Don't Tell* sales process I call the C.P.R. Sales System.

## C—Consulting (Examination Phase)

This is the examination phase where you need to ask questions specific to your customer's DRIVE and needs. Don't be a drug dealer pushing your products onto others. Ask questions so you know how to have your products solve their problems.

## P—Personalize (Diagnostic Phase)

When you are diagnosing someone's situation, the worst thing you can do is make it generic or sell them based on your DRIVE (20/80 Rule). People do not care how much you know until they know how much you care. Personalize the diagnostic phase; ask them additional questions to make sure you understand their needs. If you went in to see a doctor for a headache and they didn't ask additional questions and check your vitals, they might miss additional issues with your health. Asking inquisitive questions will help you have everything you need to recommend a product or service that will best suit their needs and DRIVE.

## R—Recommend (Prescription Phase)

Since you were listening and asking poignant questions, you know exactly how to change your standard memorized sales pitch into a custom engaging presentation that will create a Buying Bridge. The final piece of buying bridges is when you have asked and answered enough questions, thus creating a Reassociation that your customer needs your product or service.

Sales trainer extraordinaire Brian Tracy said, "Professionals who sell in the way that doctors treat patients find that their sales activities proceed far more smoothly and result in better sales in less time."

Years ago, I was filming a documentary on the speaker/author industry and had the pleasure to sit down with the legendary Les Brown. During one of the breaks he said, "Woody, if information was enough everybody would be rich, skinny, and happy. Information is not enough; people crave experiences."

Asking is an experience—telling is information. When people answer a question, they are participating in and experiencing the conversation. They feel validated by being able to share their own opinion. Telling them the benefits of your product or service is just information.

The technique of *ASK. Don't Tell* is the difference between a marriage proposal and an arranged marriage. One you want, the other you are forced to tolerate.

Do you really know what your customers want? Too often we start our conversations by telling potential clients what we think they want. However, what would happen if you started every conversation with a clean slate? Imagine you were thrust into a sales presentation and knew nothing about the audience, product, price, or timeline. How would you handle it?

"I need you at the military base right now to save this deal! It is the largest contract we have ever had. Everything depends on you."

The CEO and founder of BWI, a satellite technology company said this to Levi McPherson. Levi was hired for his unique ability in turning companies around. He had only been with the company for a week when he received the call.

He knew nothing about the military deal and was too new to have a detailed understanding about the company's offerings. With his phone smashed against his ear, he began sprinting toward his car.

"The meeting starts in fifteen minutes and I am about to get on my plane." The CEO only had enough time to give Levi the contact information for the CEO of another company they were joint venturing with on the project.

Now in his car, Levi frantically called the other CEO to find out details about the project he was supposed to save. "I'm going into surgery right now, so I won't be able to conference in during the meeting. You're on your own on this one, so don't screw it up!" The words hung in the air like a death sentence. Both companies needed this deal. However, with no access to either CEO and no time left, Levi knew he was in trouble.

"Hurry, the meeting has already started!" said the secretary as he entered the building. Not only was Levi there to save a contract he knew nothing about, now he was late. A short brunette woman with a stern jaw ushered him into a large military conference room where twelve highly decorated officers were already seated.

As he looked around the room at all of the brass, he knew two things: number one, he was clueless about the project these men wanted him to discuss in detail, and number two, he had to save this deal for the company to move forward in business. At this moment, when he felt he was about to be devoured by hungry lions, he remembered the principle: *ASK. Don't Tell.*

"Gentlemen, I'm here to represent our company. I understand there have been some frustrations on the project. What I need to find out first is what outcome you really want. So, if I was able to wave a magic wand right now, and we had everything perfect, the way that you guys wanted it, with the time frames, the delivery, the execution, the service, etc. . . what would that look like?" In the silence following his question, Levi patiently held his pen over his legal pad until the first officer spoke.

"We were promised it would be done by October but haven't heard any updates on getting started." Over the next twenty minutes, Levi proceeded to ask questions and write down answers. Through this process, he was able to identify the timeline, product, budget, deliverables, and, most importantly, the desires of the client. Impressively, he did all of this without anyone knowing he had no former knowledge of the project.

"It is my job to make this project match your goals. So, I just want to confirm, if we meet these identified deadlines and come in on budget, do we still have a deal?" Levi asked. Officers looked around the table for consent from each department head and unanimously said, "Yes." All Levi had done was repeat everything he had written down back to the officers. By following the principle of *ASK. Don't Tell,* Levi was able to create a Buying Bridge to save the largest deal his company had ever done.

Do you want to perform on stage with your favorite rock band? What about walking the red carpet at Fashion Week, even if you're a quiet banker who has never worn Prada in your life? Maybe you'd like to watch Formula 1 in Monaco with royalty. What about appear in a walk-on role on your favorite TV show? Maybe you would prefer to have a private dinner at the feet of Michelangelo's David while being serenaded by Andrea Bocelli.

These are the actual near-impossible feats that Steve Sim's company Bluefish does for his clients every day. You want to visit the International Space Station? Done. You want to play golf with a certain green jacket champion? Done. He even turned one of his clients into James Bond for a weekend. It was an incredible high-octane experience starting in Monte Carlo and ending in Moscow, complete with scantily clad women, a kidnapping by a Special Ops team, and, of course, an Aston Martin.

Bluefish is a high-end concierge service catering to the world's elite. They specialize in doing the impossible for those "who are tired of standing still, tired of the status quo, and who want to do something incredible." To achieve these life-changing experiences, Sim's team has to tap into the core of what drives people. He does this by asking questions over and over again until he gets to the core of their passion. He trains his salespeople to ask "Why" at least three times. Sims goes onto explain in his book *Bluefishing*: "The first 'why' is what they think they think, the second 'why' is what they think you want to hear, the third 'why' is what they *FEEL*." The following excerpt is from his book, demonstrating how to continue to ask questions to get to what a potential client really wants.

> Several years ago, my team got a call from a new client in New York. My people are terrific at new business calls like this, but this time my assistant put him on hold, buzzed me and said, "Look, I've got this guy on the line. There's something off. Can you jump on the call and take a listen?"
>
> I love being on the front lines as much as I can, so without hesitating I picked up the phone and said, "Hey, how are you? This is Steve Sims. How can I help you?"
>
> The voice on the phone was one of the least enthusiastic I've ever heard. Which is weird in my line of business. People call us to help make their wildest dreams happen, so usually we get people who are pretty fired up about their request.
>
> However, this guy says, in monotone, "I need to get two tickets to the Playboy Mansion."
>
> I said, "That's fine. We can make that happen for you. Let me get a pen so I can take some notes."
>
> I didn't need a pen, I needed to stall for a second, so I could think of a way to find this man's real reason for calling.
>
> So, I start chatting with him, "Have you been to the Playboy Mansion before?"
>
> "No, no I haven't." And there's still no excitement in this young man's voice about going to The Capital of Hedonism. None at all.
>
> "Do you get to Los Angeles much?" I asked, just chit-chatting.
>
> "Yeah, sometimes."
>
> "Where do you go? North? South? Just stay in the hub?"
>
> "Well, I like Hollywood, but I usually go up to Santa Barbara," and I could sense the voice was picking up in tempo.
>
> So, I said, "You like Santa Barbara?"
>
> "Oh, yeah, I love Santa Barbara."

"Really? I've been there a couple times," I commented.

"It was okay, I guess."

"What do you like so much about it?"

"Oh, well, the wine is incredible. . ." he said, and I could hear that he was smiling.

"Well, if you like wine, why aren't you heading up to Napa?" I asked.

That got him. "Oh, my God, I want to go to Napa so bad!" he said, almost like a little kid. And there it is. There's the excitement. There's the life on the line. Whew, I thought to myself, relieved. This, I can work with.

"Okay," I say, "we can send you to the Playboy Mansion, but first I really want to know why you haven't been to Napa?"

"Oh, I don't know! I always wanted to go to Napa." The guy was busting at the seams.

I thought to myself, I've got to get this guy to Napa. But I had to go through the original request protocol, so I went back to the Playboy project.

I ran through the planning for him. "We'll get you and a friend to the Playboy Mansion, you're at the Playboy Mansion for one night, let's look at your calendar."

He switched back to half-hearted right away.

When we were done scheduling, I said, "All right, back to Napa." And he perked up again. It was like flicking a switch on and off. The second I mentioned Playboy, we were in the Sh**. Mention Napa, the guy was up on cloud nine. Then it hit me. The real him came out when he was talking about Santa Barbara and Napa wine, but not about Playboy.

So, I asked, still chit-chatting, "What do you do for work?"

He said, "I'm a broker here in New York. I do this, I do that."

I said, "Got it. Now, I'm gonna go out on a limb here. And I mean no offense, and I have only acceptance, but, are girls not really your thing? And damn, mate, why the hell do you want to go to Playboy?"

He fell quiet for a moment and I thought he was going to hang up on me. I was challenging him to be authentic with me, and that's not an easy thing for people to do.

He said finally, "I get so much peer pressure. I have to do something that is pure 100 percent testosterone."

I understood. I was rolling now. He was being sincere, and so now I could sincerely help. "So, the Playboy Mansion thing is not for you," I said. "You're doing it for everyone else in your office. Just to make them think you're straight. Is that it?"

"Yeah," he said softly.

"So, you're gonna fly over to LA and spend about fifteen to twenty thousand dollars, just to hopefully placate a few assholes in your office?" I asked, incredulous.

"Apparently." He sounded defeated. I couldn't take it.

So, I said, "I've got an idea for you. We're going to send you to Napa. Because that's where your heart is. I've already got a few people going to the Playboy Mansion, so I'll get you a

> couple of ticket stubs. You'll fly back from Napa with the ticket stubs, lay them on your desk, and no one's the wiser."
>
> He was over the moon. We made that happen for him, and he became a client for many, many more years to come. Not because we sent him to Napa that one time, but because we listened to him and asked why.

Sims continues with,

> "If you can challenge your communication with someone, you in essence challenge the relationship that you'll experience as well. If you can get into that person's head and get beyond the shield, beyond the business card, beyond the pomp and ceremony, beyond the ego, beyond the fear of embarrassment, then you can deliver for them like never before. There's a person that wakes up, lives and breathes, feeds, goes to the toilet, loves their kids, and this essence is what they want. Once you can see that person, once you've got them, they don't go anywhere else. It's not because they like your flashy website, it's because you're communicating at a level they don't find anywhere else."

If you cannot get to their passion, there is no way to truly create a reassociation to be able to build the Buying Bridge.

To better understand your clients, let's take a second to analyze your passion.

- What is that one thing you love to do?
- If you had all the money and free time in the world, how would you spend it?
- If you could do anything and you knew you would not fail, what would you do?

Now, reflect on your DRIVE; you will see your passion is directly tied to whether you are a Director, Relator, Intellectual, Validator, or Executive. Imagine I had a product or service that helped you do exactly what you answered above. Wouldn't you buy it? Of course, you would; we all would.

Who has more influence, the President of the United States or a college student? Reddit.com is visited by 330 million people a month. It is ranked in the top ten most visited sites monthly. Reddit bills itself as the Front Page of The Internet. What is Reddit? Essentially, it's a massive collection of forums, where people can share news and content with others. They rank highest threads (stories) by upvotes and not by comments.

After six years of being on Reddit.com, a Questions and Answers session with then-President Barack Obama had registered 216,000 upvotes, making it the third most popular Reddit post behind #2, which was a thank you to President Obama when he left office. The #1 post was a funny meme about the proper way to upvote using Rocket and Groot from the second *Guardians of the Galaxy* film. This AMA (Ask Me Anything) with former President Obama had 23.3K comments. Anything over 1000 comments is substantial. This is why I was so shocked when I saw a no-name university student from the Rocky Mountains with 40.4K comments in under twenty-four hours. I reached out to this college student, and because of the popularity of his post, he has asked that I don't reveal his real name. For the sake of this story, I will call him Dave. What was the real difference from former President Obama and the question Dave asked?

Per my research over the last year, I have yet to see anyone come close to Dave's post in regards to engagement or participation. Maybe Dave is a genius, or maybe he cracked the viral code to get people to share and comment? Sadly, no. However, I have found the reason why his question struck a chord with people and how you can do the exact same thing for your audience. Before I reveal his question and why it worked, let me share with you the other top five questions he asked and the number of comments they received. Keep in mind these are his next top five posts under his #1 of 40,483 comments.

Thoughts on guided tours for solo travelers?
Comments: 12
Upvotes: 4

What is the best part of your morning routine?
Comments: 8
Upvotes: 3

What do you think is your best quality?
Comments: 7
Upvotes: 3

What are some good mixed drinks whose ingredients keep for a while?
Comments: 7
Upvotes: 7

What is the story behind the name you gave your car?
Comments: 2
Upvotes: 2

Here is the question that he broke the internet with:
What is a song lyric that really hits you hard?
Comments: 40,483 (in twenty-four hours)
Upvotes: 53,000

What is the difference between this one question versus his others and President Obama? He asked an emotional question. Emotional questions spark engagement, curiosity, and conversation. In your marketing when you ask emotional questions, you are creating an experience that leads to building a Buying Bridge.

Do everything in your power to stay away from "Yes" and "No" questions. For example, if you asked someone, "Are you married?" Yes or No is going to be the answer. Also, they may not be married or are going through a horrible divorce. Instead ask, "How would you describe the perfect intimate relationship?" The following questions are samples you can use to create a more meaningful conversation with your potential client's DRIVE. These are only recommendations. Customize and create your own. When you are building a Buying Bridge you need to tie your product's benefits to the challenges your potential client is facing. The second set of questions are for you to see how you can connect your product or service to their answers.

## (D) *Director*

- What was the last VIP experience you had?
  - Can your product be a VIP experience? Can it be turned into one?
- Do you prefer talking about the big picture or would you rather go through the details?
  - Can your product be a big picture solution?
- What activity makes you feel free and independent?
  - Can your product make them feel free and independent?
- Describe your perfect lifestyle.
  - Can your product enhance their lifestyle?
- When was the last time you were bored? What were you doing?
  - Can your product be exciting and entertaining?
- What is your favorite life experience?
  - Can your product connect them to a favorite life experience?
- What do you do to stay focused when the project is no longer stimulating?
  - Can your product solve their problem with losing focus?

## (R) *Relator*

- When you are making a big decision, who do you like to consult with?

- Can your product be sold when the person they refer to is present?
- What is your favorite group you like to be with?
  - Can your product support or add value to their group?
- When was the last time you exhausted yourself because you were focused on others' needs more than your own?
  - Can your product help them to recover?
- When was the last time you said, "yes" to someone when really you should have said, "no"?
  - Can your product help them organize their life so they can say "no"?
- What is your favorite thing to do to connect with others?
  - Can your product help them connect to the people they care about?
- What do you do to inspire loyalty within your community?
  - Can your product help them inspire loyalty in a community?
- What do you do to support other's dreams?
  - Can your product help them support others?

## *Intellectual* (I)

- What frustrates you the most if you do not have the right system?
  - Can your product create the right system for them?
- When you are in a group of people, what drives you crazy?
  - Can your product help them with getting along with others?
- How do you stay productive in your life, house, and business?
  - Can your product make them more productive?
- What is your method for researching the best deal?
  - Can your product help them research and get the best deal?

- How do you stay in the moment?
  - Can your product help them celebrate the moment?
- How do you stay health-conscious?
  - Can your product help them stay health-conscious?
- What is your favorite way to learn? Is it online, audio, or in books?
  - Can your product help them consume more information?

## (V) *Validator*

- What is your favorite way to validate others?
  - Can your product help them to validate others?
- What do you do when people you care about do not acknowledge your hard work?
  - Can your product help them with conflict?
- How do you like to praise and encourage others?
  - Can your product help them to encourage others?
- What do you do to find the good in people?
  - Can your product help them connect with others?
- How do you like people to show you respect and trust?
  - Can your product help them be trusted and respected?
- What do you do to be an example people want to follow?
  - Can your product help them lead a team?
- When you have a conflict with someone, how do you tend to resolve it?
  - Can your product help resolve conflict?

## (E) *Executive*

- When do you feel like you are winning?
  - Can your product help them win in their life, relationships, and business?

- When do you feel like you are in the most control?
  - Can your product help them feel more in control?
- What is your strategy for accomplishing your goals?
  - Can your product help them achieve their goals?
- How do you solve problems? What is the technique or process?
  - Can your product help them solve problems?
- When do you feel the most secure?
  - Can your product provide a sense of security?
- What is your greatest reward and your greatest challenge at work?
  - Can your product help them at work?
- What is your strategy for retirement?
  - Can your product help them with their retirement?

You want to increase your sales? Tie your product to your customer's passion—which is their DRIVE. When executed properly, you are able to build a Buying Bridge that will absolutely increase your closing ratios.

Rex Realty is one of the top real estate brokerages in their area and is run by my client, Jimmy Rex. When he learned how to close people from their personality types instead of his own, he saw his closing ratio jump from twenty-seven percent to nearly ninety-two percent. That's roughly a 340 percent increase in closings. He is on track to close 270 homes this year. I asked how he does it. He said, "After I know their DRIVE, it is easy for me to create a Reassociation. I simply curtail my pitch to match their personality."

After identifying his client's DRIVE, either through using the DRIVE Cards/Handout or the Conversation Close, he uses one of the following pitches.

"If I am trying to get the listing of the home from a Director I simply ask, 'Describe your next home to me. How do you plan on using the home? What do you like better about the new home than the old?' After I listen intently, I say, 'Great, let's list this home immediately so

you can move on to your dream home and not have to stress about this one anymore.'

"If I am trying to get the listing from a Relator, I simply ask, 'What has this home meant to you and your family? What has been your favorite part about holidays and creating memories with them? What does the new house have that will make it better for your family? If you would like me to find a family who will love and appreciate your home the way you have, I would be honored to list it and make that happen for you.'

"If I am trying to get the listing from an Intellectual, I simply ask, 'What are the features you are looking for in your new home? What have you done with your current home that you think will make it sell? Have you done a market analysis to see what you feel the home is worth?' If I know they already have, they're an Intellectual. I will then tell them that it is a huge decision and one that should not be taken lightly. I never ask for the sale with an Intellectual at the first meeting. I will give them a packet of information on my company and our services as well as premade market analysis on their home to review with current comps. Then I ask, 'After you have had time to review this material, what would be a good day for me to follow up about listing your home?'

"If I am trying to get a listing from a Validator, I simply ask, 'So what has been your favorite part of owning this house?' As we walk through the home, I authentically (and it has to be authentic) compliment them on the different color choices and upgrades they have made throughout the house. I have them describe to me what they want their next house to be like and compliment their ideas—once again authentically. Then I say, 'Well, let's not hold you up from showing your family and friends your new dream home. When would you like me to list the home?'

"If I am trying to get a listing from an Executive, I will say, 'What features in your home do you feel will sell this quickly? What has to be done to make it more sellable than your neighbors?' (Knowing they are driven to win and have control, I know they already know the answers to these questions.) After listening intently and taking notes I will say, 'To make sure I understand you properly . . .' and then I repeat the points we have talked about. Finally, I will comment, 'Then I feel your property is worth X and if you are confident with that number I can have it listed in twenty-four hours.'"

What Jimmy does so eloquently on each sales presentation is to create a Reassociation from his services to his customer's DRIVE. This builds a Buying Bridge.

*To build the ultimate Buying Bridge, do the following:*

1. Identify their DRIVE (See Chapter 7)
2. Ask the questions specific to their DRIVE (C.P.R. Sales System)
3. Keep asking questions (ASK—Always Seek Knowledge)—resolving concerns until the reassociation happens. In that moment ask for the sale. That completes the Buying Bridge.

Sometimes when you are building your Buying Bridge, you come across a situation when you really need to get someone's attention, or it may be a group of people. In those moments use *SHOW. Don't Tell.*

10

## SHOW. Don't Tell.

With $1 billion on the line, Jon Stegner had an enormous challenge to create a Reassociation for top management. He saw an opportunity to cut purchasing costs by two percent, which would save over a billion dollars in five years. He had to sell the idea, but for the most part, he did not know how to convince the top brass to change their buying behavior to get the desired result. In *The Heart of Change* by John P. Kotter and Dan S. Cohen, they share the story of Stegner and this incredible process of subtle persuasion.

To get a sense of the magnitude of the problem, Stegner asked one of their summer interns to do a small study of how much the company pays for gloves used in their factories and how many different gloves they buy. He chose one product to keep it simple, something all the plants used and something they could all easily relate to.

When the intern completed the project, she reported their factories were purchasing 424 different kinds of gloves. Four hundred and twenty-four! Every factory had its own supplier and its own negotiated price. The same glove could cost $5.00 at one factory and $17.00 at another. The intern was able to collect a sample of every one of the 424 gloves. She tagged each one with the price and the factory it was used in.

To create the greatest impact, Stegner reserved the executive conference room and placed all the gloves, tagged with each price, on the table, creating a small mountain of overpriced samples. Then he invited all the division presidents to come visit the room. What they saw was a large, expansive table, normally clean or organized with a few papers; now it was stacked high with gloves. Each of the executives stared at this display for a minute.

Then they said something like, "We buy all these different kinds of gloves?"

"Well, as a matter of fact, yes, we do."

"Really?"

"Yes, really."

Then they walked around the table. Browsing the pile, they began to look for the gloves that their factories were using. They looked at two gloves that seemed exactly alike, yet one was marked $3.22 and the other $10.55.

It was a rare event when these executives didn't have anything to say. But that day, they just stood with their mouths gaping.

This demonstration quickly gained notoriety. The gloves became part of a traveling roadshow. They went to every division. They went to dozens of plants. Many people had the opportunity to look at the stacks of gloves. The roadshow reinforced at every level of the organization a sense of "this is how bad it is." This small, subtle technique that created such a massive change in the organization is called *SHOW. Don't Tell.* Stegner could have emailed all of the executives a spreadsheet with the exact comparison of numbers, but would that have created any change? He could have made an illuminating PowerPoint with animation, pictures, and graphs, but what would that have really done? *SHOW. Don't Tell* creates an experience, not just more information.

*SHOW. Don't Tell.* can be remembered by the acronym of S.H.O.W.

S—Social Proof

H—Hands On

O—Offer Samples

W—Wow Factor

As you walk down any street in any major city in the world, you will see retail stories with window displays clamouring for your attention. In the late 1800s, Macy's in New York started this tradition, but it wasn't until Gene Moore of Tiffany & Co. that it made a real difference. He is credited for making Tiffany a brand and designing over five thousand window displays. How did he do it? **Contrast.** When designing a window, he would have crystal wine goblets organized on a table with one broken on the floor, or he would place twelve knives in a row with one facing the wrong way. Often individuals would be walking by, spot the "mistake," then walk into Tiffany's and ask to speak to the manager, letting them know there was something wrong with their window display. The manager would say, "Thank you for letting us know. Have you seen our new necklaces?" or whatever they were marketing that week. It was Moore's way of knowing if people were paying attention. In the *SHOW. Don't Tell* Playbook, the greater the contrast the greater the engagement. Does your product or service have a *SHOW. Don't Tell* element? Does it stop someone in their tracks?

Visualize a juicy hamburger in your mind. Did you see the spelling of "J-u-i-c-y H-a-m-b-u-r-g-e-r", or did you visualize a mouth-watering hamburger with all the toppings and a butter-toasted bun? If you are like most people, then you "SEE" the hamburger and not the spelling of the word hamburger. This is why *SHOW. Don't Tell* is so crucial. The more visual and experimental your product or sales process can be, the greater the impression can imprint on the mind while creating a lasting effect.

This was never more apparent than in the groundbreaking research and book *Buy-ology* by Martin Lindstrom. During a three-year neuromarketing study, they peered into the brains of 2000 volunteers around the world as they encountered various ads, logos, commercials, brands, and products to see how marketing affected the brain.

Did you know by the time you are sixty-six years old, you will have seen two million television commercials, according to Lindstrom? That's the equivalent of watching eight hours of ads seven days a week for six years straight. The average consumer in 1965 could recall thirty-four percent of the ads they had seen. In 1990, it dropped to eight percent. By 2007, ACNielsen found after interviewing 1000 people that it dropped to 2.21 percent. Imagine how low it is now with the constant bombardment of ads from your social media apps, news sites, games, and television.

Two industry titans were fighting for viewer recall at the launch of *American Idol* on a warm summer day—June 11th, 2002. Both Coca-Cola and the Ford Motor Company paid a premium $26 million to be title sponsors of this unproven singing talent show. On *American Idol*, Coke not only ran thirty-second ads during commercial breaks, they also featured their products prominently during the show itself. This was a *SHOW. Don't Tell* tactic. The three judges kept cups of America's most iconic soft drink in front of them, and both the judges and the contestants sat on chairs or couches with rounded contours specifically designed to look like a bottle of Coca-Cola. Before and after their auditions, contestants entered a room whose walls were painted a chirpy, unmistakable Coca-Cola red. Whether through semi-subtle imagery or traditional advertising spots, Coca-Cola is present approximately sixty percent of the time on *American Idol*.

The other key sponsor, Ford, does not share in the design of the show. It traditionally stayed with just their thirty-second ads.

Lindstrom and the doctors selected 400 random volunteers and hooked them up to an SST brain-scanning machine that would reveal how different ads connect with the brain. This would allow them to see how the brain recalls certain images (the ads). The subjects were shown random ads from Coke and Ford as well as other companies. Then the same subjects watched snippets from *American Idol* with their ads. What they wanted to know was if Coke, with its SHOW. Don't Tell strategy, and Ford, with its traditional ads only, had any impact on product recall.

So, what was the result? In the first test of branded and unbranded ads, the recall was roughly the same. Meaning the subjects recalled Ford and Coke at the same pace as other random ads. However, when compared to the ads and snippets from *American Idol* where Coke is integrated into the show and the Ford ads that were not intergraded, the comparison was drastic. Coke saw a measurably higher recall. Ford did not fare so well. The Ford Company paid $26 million and actually lost market share. When being questioned about the ads, the subjects remembered an automobile company but not which one. Through the *SHOW. Don't Tell* Process, the more you can integrate your product into the "SHOW" process, the more it will stay with consumers.

## *SHOW. Don't Tell*—Social Proof

The Rolls Royce Bespoke Dealership in Abu Dhabi is the number one dealership in the world. When you walk into Kidhim H.H. Al Helli's office, you will notice something unique behind his desk. As manager, he showcases his trophies for being top in sales. He believes these awards position him in front of his prospective clients as being number one.

Kidhim is not off at all. Social Proof is one of the six principles of influence identified by Robert Cialdini in his book *Influence—The Psychology of Persuasion.* Think back to the fundraiser phenomenon, the Ice Bucket Challenge in 2014. During this viral video challenge, people would film themselves pouring an ice bucket over their heads and calling out other people to donate to the ALS foundation. The major driver was Social Proof. As friends called out friends and celebrities called out other celebrities, there were over 2.2 million videos made within the first thirty days. Traditionally the annual donations raised by the ALS foundation was $2.5 million. Within sixty days of this social proof campaign they raised over $115 million.

On a Friday night, while trying to decide what movie to see, the average person will turn to Rotten Tomatoes or other social platforms to choose a movie. This Social Proof helps one make a better decision. Cialdini identified three main reasons why Social Proof has such a strong impact.

1. Social Proof is one of the main gauges people use to decide or to believe in, based on what other people are doing or believing.
2. People are more likely to rely on Social Proof when there is uncertainty (they don't know what decision to make).
3. Social Proof is most influential when there is similarity: the herd mentality. If you see others like you acting a certain way you are more likely to act the same way. (e.g., Ice Bucket Challenge)

To customers, Five Guys is best known as a no-frills, dependably satisfying burger chain with a red-and-white aesthetic and a minimalist menu. When you walk into any Five Guys, whether you are at

Piccadilly Circus in the heart of London or on Wilshire Boulevard in Los Angeles, you will notice one consistent thing: the walls are plastered with Social Proof—third-party validation. On the restaurant walls, hang dozens of magazine articles showcasing their amazing burgers. They use this Social Proof as part of their corporate theme and decorations.

According to David Griner from *Adweek*, "Since being founded in Washington, D.C., in 1986, the brand has balked at paid ads, focusing instead on its in-store experience and, as it grew across the nation and then the globe, the publicity boost each time it expanded into a new market. Today the company has 1,551 locations across 12 countries and continues to expand at a pace of roughly 100 new locations per year."

Without Social Proof, crowdfunding companies like Kickstarter.com or Indiegogo.com would not exist. Budding inventors and entrepreneurs would have fewer places to explore their opportunities. The secret success behind crowdfunding is how Social Proof brings others to the project. For example, one of the top 10 projects on Kickstarter is the Exploding Kittens card game. "A card game for people who are into kittens and explosions."

It used Social Proof to attract 219,382 backers who raised $8,782,571 in thirty days. This unique specialty niche game would never have made it on the shelf of traditional retail, but after the success of their campaign, you can find it at Target and Walmart as well as other big-box retailers. The Coolest Cooler, a Frankenstein product combining a drink cooler and margarita blender, raised $13,285,226 from 62,642 backers. According to *Forbes,* crowding funding has skyrocketed to $32 billion in 2018.

In my own business, I saw the importance of Social Proof while negotiating a significant contract to consult with a large sales company. The CEO (a Validator) and I had built a relationship over a couple of years; I hosted him and his top brass in my home to go over some strategies. We had agreed upon a price, and I was simply waiting for a signed contract when suddenly the CEO was hesitating on moving forward. Upon further discovery, I found out his VP (an Executive) wanted verification (Proof) of my expertise. I was on the road when I got the call asking if I could email him a list of over 200 video and written testimonials. Without those testimonials I would never have gotten the contract. Whether you are dealing with a Director, Relator, Intellectual, Validator, or Executive, Social Proof supports what motivates their decision-making process. The key is matching the Social Proof you have to their DRIVE.

## *SHOW. Don't Tell*—Hands On

Here is a tale of two companies, both started in the 1890s. Their products are widely distributed and known around the world. Both have even made it into outer space among products used at the International Space Station. One is a giant, international, school-yard bully, dominating on every front. The other seems to be the short, mismatched runt who gets picked second every time and can't get any respect. After roughly seventy years of business, the giant had sales of $568 million with profits of $47 million. The runt had worked extremely hard with aggressive marketing to close the gap with sales of $192 million and profits of only $15 million. There was no comparison between the two.

A strange thing happened the following decade. This underdog created a cutting-edge *SHOW. Don't Tell* public marketing campaign called the "Pepsi Challenge." In 1975, the Pepsi Company set up a "Hands-On" blind sampling between Pepsi-Cola and rival Coca-Cola. During these blind taste tests, the majority of participants picked Pepsi as the better tasting of the two soft drinks. PepsiCo took great advantage of the campaign with television commercials reporting the results

to the public. Embracing their new self-image, they launched a new marketing slogan, the "Pepsi Generation." They were positioning Coke as a stale old company. Ironically, there was nothing new or hip about either one; they were both eighty-year-old companies.

This technique of *SHOW. Don't Tell* with a Hands On experience changed the course of Pepsi's future. With their new-found success, they diversified over the next two decades, acquiring brands such as Pizza Hut, Taco Bell, KFC, Hot 'n Now, Mountain Dew, Lay's, Gatorade, Tropicana, 7 Up, Doritos, Brisk, Quaker Foods, and Cheetos. They have since spun off some of these properties into different companies. What was the outcome from their Hands On experiment and brand acquisitions? Sales exceed $63 billion with profits of $4.8 billion. Contrast this with Coca-Cola, whose sales are $35 billion with $1.2 billion in profits. Coke may have won the cola wars, but Pepsi won the revenue war.

A client of mine, Studies Weekly, competes in the high pressure-tight budget elementary education system. Their product is unique because they don't publish textbooks; instead, they publish weekly newspapers from Social Studies to English. The newspapers are interactive for each student. I was brought into strategize DRIVE for their sales pitches. They typically meet with a group of teachers, principals, and school board leaders. The sales process is very tedious and competitive. To stand out and create a Reassociation, one of the salespeople shared with me a technique he uses which falls under "Hands On." Instead of giving everyone a standard PowerPoint pitch, he pulls out newspapers, scissors, paste, and tape. He actually has the faculty go through a class lesson by cutting up the newspaper and role playing. Instantly, the teachers and leaders see how to use the product instead of being told how to. This technique helped increase their sales by forty-two percent.

Think of the car industry. How would sales be if you couldn't test drive a car? As you walk into any computer electronic store or cell phone carrier there are displays of their newest devices for you to try out. Think about the offers where you get to spend three days and two nights in an exotic location if you are willing to spend ninety minutes on a timeshare presentation. These Hands On experiences propel sales for these industries.

I cut my teeth in business at the age of sixteen going to tradeshows sourcing products and then finding new marketing strategies to increase sales. To this day, if I hear of a renaissance festival, home & garden show, or any trade show, I am the first in line to attend. I am looking for those one or two individuals who have a crowd around their booth. They are creating a "Hands On" experience. It is like stepping into a live infomercial. They have milliseconds to get someone's attention. We have all seen the opposite, a booth with a banner and guy or gal is sitting there with their business cards on the table and a bowl of candy waiting to have someone to talk to. You walk right on by as if they have some contagious boredom disease you are trying to avoid. But then there is an individual who has a new and improved mop that twists and shakes all the dirt and grime from your floors. They have a headset on and there is usually a mirror above their heads so when the crowd forms, and it will, those standing in the back can still see.

But what if you don't have a product that is Hands On, like mortgages, insurance, or any professional service? One of my clients came to me with this dilemma. They wanted to do the tradeshow circuit but wanted to stand out. It was during the presidential election for Donald Trump and Hillary Clinton. I had them set up their booth with two life-size cardboard cut-outs of Trump and Clinton. They bought ten Nerf guns and two thousand Nerf darts and put a sign above that said, "Who Do You Want To Win? Take your best shot." People stopped and lined up to take shots. The crowd formed and their business exploded. The dart exercise had nothing to do with their business. It was a Hands On experience to get people to stop and talk.

How can you make your product more Hands On? Can you create a "Try Before You Buy" scenario? Think about Apple and their store layout. When you walk into an Apple store the entire layout is designed to be a Hands On experience. Even their packaging for their phone covers slips on and off so you can try your phone cover on before you buy. If your product is an intangible, what other Hands On experience can you create to get people's attention? Amazon allows you to preview a small section of a book before you buy. Look for ways to add a Hands On element to your product and you will see your sales increase.

## *SHOW. Don't Tell*—Offer Samples

When you are taking a sample at a store, how many is too many? What is the proper threshold for raviolis? Is there a cutoff point for cheese cubes on toothpicks? Just ask Erwin Lingitz, a sixty-eight-year-old Minnesota retiree who was allegedly "jumped, kicked, and beaten" when he took 1.4 pounds of beef sticks and summer sausages that had been laid out as free samples at Cub Foods in White Bear Township. He was arrested for violating "societal norms and common customer understanding regarding free-sample practices."

Maybe his enthusiasm got the best of him. But who doesn't like a free sample? When offered a sample, three out of four people will accept the offer according to a new study. Retail giant Costco has been offering samples for years. According to Giovanni DeMeo of the product-demonstration company Interactions, a department of which handles Costco's samples:

> When we compare it to other in-store mediums . . . in-store product demonstration has the highest [sales] lift, the short-term spike in sales isn't the only effect of product sampling that matters—it's great for making customers loyal to stores and brands over longer periods of time—the figures are impressive. In the past year, Interactions' beer samples at many national retailers on average boosted sales by 71 percent, and its samples of frozen pizza increased sales by 600 percent.

The effect of giving out samples operate on a more subconscious level. "Reciprocity is a very, very strong instinct," says Dan Ariely, a behavioral economist at Duke University. "If somebody does something for you"—such as giving you a quarter of a ravioli on a piece of wax paper—"you really feel a rather surprisingly strong obligation to do something back for them."

Ariely adds that free samples can make forgotten cravings become more prominent. "What samples do is they give you a particular desire for something," he says. "If I gave you a tiny bit of chocolate, all of a sudden it would remind you about the exact taste of chocolate and would increase your craving."

When Snack Factory launched the unknown and untested Pretzel Crisps, the only way to get people to try it was by offering free samples of its flat pretzel cracker to reach both pretzel and chip lovers. According to Perry Abbenante, Snack Factory vice president of marketing, the conversion rate of the sampling efforts was between twenty-five and thirty percent, meaning that at least a quarter of those who tried a free sample ended up buying the product.

When using Offer Samples as a *SHOW. Don't Tell.* Strategy, this can benefit both you and your customers by:

- Building brand loyalty with existing customers
- Introducing your product or services to a new audience
- Enhancing knowledge of your product or service
- Bringing brand awareness to an audience unfamiliar with your business
- Promoting a big event

## *SHOW. Don't Tell*—Wow Factor

With a *SHOW. Don't Tell.*–Wow Factor strategy, you get to use a technique that is creative and, if done properly, can be jaw-dropping. Chip and Dan Heath illustrate this with the following story from their book *Made To Stick.*

> Art Silverman stared at a bag of movie popcorn. It looked out of place sitting on his desk. His office had long since filled up with fake butter fumes. Silverman knew, because of his organization's research, that the popcorn on his desk was unhealthy. Shockingly unhealthy, in fact. His job was to figure out a way to communicate this message to the unsuspecting moviegoers of America.
>
> Silverman worked for the Center for Science in the Public Interest (CSPI), a non-profit group that educates the public about nutrition. The CSPI sent bags of movie popcorn from a dozen theaters in three major cities to a lab for nutritional analysis. The results surprised everyone.
>
> The United States Department of Agriculture (USDA) recommends that a normal diet contain no more than twenty grams of saturated fat each day. According to the lab results, the typical bag of popcorn had thirty-seven grams.

The culprit was coconut oil, which theaters used to pop their popcorn. Coconut oil had some big advantages over other oils. It gave the popcorn a nice, silky texture, and released a more pleasant and natural aroma than the alternative oils. Unfortunately, as the lab results showed, coconut oil was also brimming with saturated fat.

The single serving of popcorn on Silverman's desk—a snack someone might scarf down between meals—had nearly two days' worth of saturated fat. And those thirty-seven grams of saturated fat were packed into a medium-sized serving of popcorn. No doubt a decent sized bucket could have cleared triple digits.

The challenge, Silverman realized, was that few people know what "thirty-seven grams of saturated fat" means. Most of us don't memorize the USDA's daily nutrition recommendations. Is thirty-seven grams good or bad? And even if we have an intuition that it's bad, we'd wonder if it was "bad bad" (like cigarettes) or "normal bad" (like a cookie or a milk shake).

Even the phrase "thirty grams of saturated fat" by itself was enough to cause most people's eyes to glaze over. "Saturated fat has zero appeal," Silverman says. "It's dry, it's academic, who cares?" Silverman could have created some kind of visual comparison-perhaps an advertisement comparing the amount of saturated fat in the popcorn with the USDA's recommended daily allowance. Think of a bar graph, with one of the bars stretching twice as high as the other.

But that was too scientific somehow. Too rational. The amount of fat in this popcorn was, in some sense, not rational. It was ludicrous. The CSPI needed a way to shape the message in a way that fully communicated this ludicrousness.

Silverman came up with a solution.

CSPI called a press conference on September 27, 1992. Here's the message it presented: "A medium-sized 'butter' popcorn at a

typical neighborhood movie theater contains more artery-clogging fat than a bacon-and-eggs breakfast, a Big Mac and fries for lunch, and a steak dinner with all the trimmings—combined!"

The folks at CSPI didn't neglect the visuals—they laid out the full buffet of greasy food for the television cameras. An entire day's worth of unhealthy eating, displayed on a table. All that saturated fat stuffed into a single bag of popcorn.

The story was an immediate sensation, featured on CBS, NBC, ABC, and CNN. It made the front pages of USA Today, the Los Angeles Times, and The Washington Post's Style section. Night show host Leno and Letterman cracked jokes about fat-soaked popcorn, and headline writers trotted out some doozies: "Popcorn Gets an 'R' Rating," "Lights, Action, Cholesterol!" "Theater Popcorn is Double Feature of Fat."

The idea stuck. Moviegoers, repulsed by these findings, avoided popcorn in droves. Sales plunged. The service staff at movie houses grew accustomed to fielding questions about whether the popcorn was popped in the "bad" oil. Soon after, most of the nation's biggest theater chains—including United Artists, AMC, and Loews-announced that they would stop using coconut oil.

For the Center for Science in the Public Interest to shock moviegoers to change their behavior, a *SHOW. Don't Tell* technique worked perfectly. How can you use this strategy for your customers? What are the benefits of your product? How can you "Show" them?

Would you ever put a wood 2x2 board into a blender, just to see if it blended? Most likely, you wouldn't. This was exactly what George Wright was thinking as he walked past the CEO Tom Dickson as he was feeding a 2x2 into the company's blender.

Wright is the VP of marketing for Blendtec Blenders. The company sells one of the most uninteresting and over-saturated commodities in any department store. Blenders are largely all the same; many times consumers will not be able to recall a specific brand let alone be convinced to buy a particular model. Blendtec, therefore, needed to differentiate its product strategy to increase brand awareness and thus its market share.

Wright found the destruction test the CEO was doing fascinating and thought others might, too. With only a $50 marketing budget they created both an *ASK. Don't Tell* and a *SHOW. Don't Tell* campaign.

Immediately, Wright gathered his webmaster and his video producer, who usually made boring instructional and maintenance videos. They spent the $50 on a domain, a lab coat, pair of safety glasses, a bag of marbles, a twelve-pack of Diet Coke, a McDonald's Happy Meal, a rotisserie chicken, and a garden rake. Then they went to the

©Courtesy Photo

CEO and asked him to blend each of the items they had purchased on camera.

The ad campaign was built around a Wow Factor (*SHOW. Don't Tell.*) and a question (*ASK. Don't Tell.*) "Will It Blend?". By asking this question, Blendtec's sales skyrocketed. Their "Will It Blend?" videos became the 33rd-most-viewed series on YouTube, helping drive sales of the company's $400 high-end consumer blender up by 500 percent in 2008. Their website has seen a 650 percent increase in viewership, pushing sales over the 50 million–dollar mark.

Dickson has gone on to film sixty-two other "Will It Blend?" videos, blending everything from Bic lighters and a video camera to an iPhone and golf balls. Some of Blendtec's videos have gone viral, including "Will an iPad Blend?", which exceeded seventeen million views, and Glow Sticks, which received eleven million views.

In fact, so popular is this worldwide phenomenon that 210,000 people logged on to eBay to view the leftovers of a blended iPod and iPhone. The dust of each of these products fetched $800 and $901 respectively.

To create your *SHOW. Don't Tell* strategy, tie it back to your customer's DRIVE. Listed below are key motivators that engage each DRIVE.

### *S.H.O.W. Don't Tell*

S.—Social Proof
H.—Hands On
O.—Offer Samples
W.—Wow Factor

### *Director* (D)

- Lifestyle driven
- Experiences
- Visually stimulating

- Fun, free-spirited, creative
- Engaging not technical

### (R) Relator

- Customer experiences
- How it will help their community
- Service-oriented
- Help them lead more people
- How it gives back

### (I) Intellectual

- Step-by-step processes
- Saves time and money
- Clear and precisely communicated
- Credible source
- How it enhances their knowledge

### (V) Validator

- Makes them look like a rock star
- Will have a positive impact on others
- Helps them build their teams
- Enhances communication, trust, and attention
- Brings positive focus to them

### (E) Executive

- Third-party testimonials
- Social proof of actual clients
- Clear vision on how they will win

- People who have achieved their goals using your product
- How your products solved a client's problem

To increase your sales and your conversion ratios, identify the benefits of your products. Then pair those benefits with the proper DRIVE to create a Reassociation. The two best techniques to build a Buying Bridge are *ASK. Don't Tell* and *SHOW. Don't Tell.* But what happens if you have done everything right and they still don't buy? Then you need P.I.C.K.S.

11

# How to Save the Sale with P.I.C.K.S.

Every sale is a locked box of opportunity for you and your potential client. Sometimes after you have done everything right, the sale still does not go through. To unlock that box, you need to use lock P.I.C.K.S. When you get stuck, P.I.C.K.S. is designed to help you overcome hurdles and objections. When you cannot get through to someone, use one of the following:

*P.I.C.K.S.*

P—Parables
I—Identify Needs
C—Call to Action
K—Keep in Touch
S—Surprise Them

## P.I.C.K.S.—Parables: The Profit is in the Parables

How many times in sales training have we heard "Facts Tell—Stories Sell"? To prove this, Joshua Glenn and Rob Walker decided to do a social experiment. They bought two hundred trinkets at local thrift stores with prices ranging from $0.50 to $1.45. Then they enlisted two hundred writers to create fake stories around each object. Now they

were ready to test their hypothesis. Each trinket and story went onto eBay to be auctioned off. The results were jaw-dropping. The hand-carved wooden apple that was purchased for a dollar sold for $105. The ceramic Native American doll purchased for $0.99 was sold for $157.50. What is the value of a story? In total, they spent $125 on trinkets and grossed over $8000, a 6700 percent return on investment.

Depending on which DRIVE you are addressing, you want to use a specific story to help create the final Reassociation to make a deal happen. Here are five stories—one for each DRIVE you could use to save the sale. Please customize these stories to fit your needs and situation.

**Director:** The pain was excruciating. He lay still, trying to collect his thoughts. The sound of crushing metal and the feeling of being thrown from the front window of the plane replayed in his head. He wondered if he was going to make it out alive. As he surveyed the flipped plane, he tried to figure out what went wrong on his first day of flying lessons.

This was not the first time Bill had failed at something. He was a gifted mechanic and inventor but by the age of thirty-two he had made and lost many fortunes. One of his greatest inventions was

the Majestic Radio, the first popular mass-produced radio for the home. It was also his idea to condense the radio and install it in cars. Lacking the financial backing to pursue this dream, Bill had to make ends meet, so he sold the idea to the Galvin Manufacturing Company, which later changed their name to Motorola. He missed out on a financial landslide that would have made him independently wealthy.

One day, while seeing planes soar above him, he decided to tap into his lifelong passion for aviation. It was this passion which caused the near-fatal accident. In Chicago he worked for free as an airplane mechanic just so he could be around planes and to have the opportunity to take flying lessons. Never quitting or backing down, he mastered all the instruments and became an accomplished pilot.

Eventually he bought his own biplane. While flying he saw the need for aircraft radios. Starting from scratch, he made and successfully sold his radios to pilots. His operations moved from Chicago to New York, and within three months of the move his business failed. Still driven to create and build things, he developed a radio frequency amplifier that could be fitted to existing radios and allowed pilots to have a longer range of communication. Within five years of his last business failure, RCA made him an offer he could not refuse. He started a manufacturing company to produce aircraft instruments.

The new company exploded with success, employing 1800 people, including an additional 300 scientists and engineers. Their inventions included an automatic piloting device for fighter jets as well as communication devices for satellites.

While vacationing in Europe, Bill was intrigued by a story he heard about an attempt to make small commercial jets. A company in Switzerland canceled the project they had been working on when their first two experimental planes crashed.

When he presented his idea to the board of directors, the aviation experts did not debate whether it would work. The debate was about how long it would take him to fail.

It was public knowledge that a small-scaled jet could not be made. In his frustration he would often say, "For crying out loud, try something!"

The demand for large corporate jets was already being serviced by many competitors, so Bill saw an opportunity to develop his own niche. He was expected to fail because even if he were to get 300 orders over the next seven years for his "baby jets" it would still not be enough to make the company profitable.

At the age of sixty, when most people are thinking about retiring, Bill was still driven as an entrepreneur to create the impossible, so he sold his company's stock for millions and put his entire life savings into his dream.

He was given approval for creating the small commercial jets from the Federal Aviation Administration within eighteen months of starting his new company. This feat alone was unheard of, and it shocked everyone in the industry; everyone, that is, except Bill Lear.

In fact, Lear Jets did $52 million their first year on the market. It didn't take long for people and corporations to begin lining up for Bill's "baby jets." Today a Lear jet is considered the best of the best. It is the plane of choice for corporations, billionaires, dignitaries, and celebrities.

### How to use this story with a DIRECTOR (D)

Directors are motivated by *Lifestyle* and being free to live the way they want. Do the benefits of your product or services help them achieve a desired lifestyle? As you ask these questions and others, make sure the answer is you or your product.

- Bill Lear failed at other opportunities before he finally created the lifestyle he wanted. How can I help you overcome your current challenges?
- Like Bill, at some point you have to say, "For crying out loud, try something!" Are you ready to try something new?
- When you are creating your dream, the experts are going to bet against you. Double down and invest in yourself. Are you ready to bet on yourself?

**Relator:** The world would not be the same without Narnia and Middle Earth. The alternate universes that authors C.S. Lewis and J.R.R. Tolkien created are beloved by generations of readers and moviegoers. Lewis and Tolkien are two of the best-selling authors of all time. However, these two men may never have written their books if not for the legendary friendship they shared. Lewis and Tolkien were both professors at Oxford University. They were founding members of a writing club called Inklings. One night in September 1931, Lewis and Tolkien took a walk to discuss their combined passion for writing. It changed their lives as well as those who would read their works.

C.S. Lewis was a very rational man. He was raised in the Church of Ireland but fell away from it during his teenage years, unable to reconcile the tenets of the Church with his intellect. As an adult, Lewis found his faith again as an Anglican but struggled with how to incorporate his imagination with his faith. Lewis struggled to bring his imaginative side and his rational side together. His rational side

told him that while his stories may be entertaining, they didn't teach the reader anything that really mattered. Tolkien helped Lewis bring peace to his two sides—the reason and the imagination—together. Tolkien stirred the imagination of Lewis and stoked the flames of his intellect. Suddenly it was clear. Lewis could see how he could weave the themes of his faith into his stories and both entertain and enlighten his readers. *The Chronicles of Narnia* was born.

And what did Lewis's friendship do for Tolkien? Can you conceive of a world without *The Lord of the Rings*? Without Lewis's influence, very few people would ever have read the story of the one true ring. Tolkien was a very private man. When he and Lewis became friends, he had written part of his mythic tale of Middle Earth but had only shared it with a private audience of trusted friends. Tolkien did not have the confidence to publish his stories. He believed no one would be interested in them. From the very beginning of their friendship, Lewis encouraged his friend Tolkien to finish his epic trilogy and publish it. Lewis brought out Tolkien's confidence. The result was *The Lord of the Ring* trilogy.

Without their friendship, Lewis and Tolkien may have gone down in history as two beloved professors in Oxford's English department rather than two of the greatest writers of all time. Lewis might never have given us Narnia and Tolkien may never have introduced us to Gandalf. They supported and enriched each other as men and as writers and inspired each other to be greater than they would have been alone.

### *How to use this story with a RELATOR* (R)

Relators are motivated by *Community*. Do the benefits of your product or services help them connect with their community? As you ask these questions and others, make sure the answer is you or your product.

- Who is your Tolkien or Lewis? Do you need someone to support you? I am here to help you be more successful.
- You don't want to leave this world with your greatest work in you. How can I support your dreams?
- To be more successful do you feel you need an accountability partner?

**Intellectual:** One of the most common causes of failure is the habit of quitting when one is overtaken by temporary defeat. Every person is guilty of this mistake at one time or another. In Napoleon Hill's book *Think and Grow Rich* he tells the story of R. U. Darby's uncle who was caught by the "gold fever" during the western migration of the gold rush. He staked a claim and went to work with a pick and shovel. The going was hard, but his lust for gold was definite.

After weeks of labor, he was rewarded by the discovery of the shining ore. He needed machinery to bring the ore to the surface. Quietly, he covered up the mine, retraced his footsteps to his home in Williamsburg, Maryland, and told his relatives and a few neighbors of the "strike." They got together money for the needed machinery and had it shipped. The uncle and Darby went back to work the mine.

The first car of ore was mined and shipped to a smelter. The returns proved they had one of the richest mines in Colorado. A few more cars of that ore would clear their debts. Then the remaining gold would be all profits.

Down went the drills. Up went the hopes of Darby and his uncle. Then something happened: The vein of gold ore disappeared. They had come to the end of the rainbow, and the pot of gold was no longer there. They drilled on, desperately trying to pick up the vein again—all to no avail.

Finally, they decided to quit. They sold the machinery to a junk man for a few hundred dollars and took the train back home. This junk man called in a mining engineer to look at the mine and do a little calculating. The engineer advised the project had failed because the owners were not familiar with "fault lines." His calculations showed that the vein would be found again *just three feet* from where the Darbys had stopped drilling. And that is exactly where it was found.

The junk man took millions of dollars in ore from the mine because he knew enough to seek expert counsel before giving up.

## *How to use this story with an INTELLECTUAL*

Intellectuals are motivated by *Systems*. Do the benefits of your product or services help them create a better system? As you ask these questions and others, make sure the answer is you or your product.

- Are you three feet from gold? Do you have the right system in place to help you find your success?
- When do you feel like quitting? What are your symptoms? What is your backup plan to keep going?
- When you get stuck, how do you get unstuck?

**Validator:** On April 1st, 1976, a small computer company called Apple Inc. was founded in Cupertino, California. Most of us know the company had two co-founders named Steve Jobs and Steve Wozniak. But did you know that there was a third co-founder? This little-known guy provided all the money and early business expertise enabling Apple to get off the ground. And in return for taking a chance on two unproven entrepreneurs, this third founder was given a ten percent equity stake in the company. So why has most of the world never heard of this guy? Has he been too busy over the last few decades sipping Mai-Tais and traveling the world with supermodels on his private jet? Well, not exactly. Unfortunately, not long after co-founding what would eventually become one of the most valuable companies in the world, the third co-founder wound up making the worst decision in business history.

In fact, just twelve days after forming the company with Wozniak and Jobs, Ronald Wayne decided to sell his entire stake back for the measly sum of $2300. That is right, $2300. His reason? He just didn't want to take the risk. He didn't believe these two unproven entrepreneurs could be successful. Today a ten percent stake in Apple would be worth $100 billion. Mr. Wayne has since retired and lives in a mobile home in rural Nevada.

## Ⓥ *How to use this story with a VALIDATOR*

Validators are motivated by *Admiration*. Do the benefits of your product or services help them achieve admiration for their teams or themselves? As you ask these questions and others, make sure the answer is you or your product.

- Is there part of your life you are running from when you should actually be doubling down and being more committed?
- Are you currently trusting yourself and your ability to succeed? How can I support you?
- In your current endeavors, when you succeed, unlike Ronald Wayne, what will your family or friends say?

**Executive:** When Conrad was growing up, he wanted to be like his dad, a successful entrepreneur who owned many businesses in their small town. However, when his father found him sleeping in past

7:00 a.m. one day, he labeled him as a "lazy oaf who would never amount to anything." Conrad refused to believe this label applied to him; he became very driven with a winning mindset and a disciplined work ethic. He threw himself into his education and entered politics after graduation, winning a seat in the state legislature of New Mexico. After serving two years in politics, he persuaded his father to open a bank with him. He started as a teller and within a couple of years worked his way up to become bank president. Upon earning this position, Conrad tried to buy the bank from his father, but he refused.

Wanting to break out on his own, he looked for a different bank to buy. He had enough connections in the industry to borrow the necessary funds. After two barely missed opportunities to buy a small bank, he went to Cisco, Texas, where a banker was selling one. Conrad did not negotiate the price because he had already been out-bid twice before. The seller took Conrad's speedy offer as an impression he might be selling it for too little, so he quickly raised the price, which frustrated Conrad. He went to the local hotel to find a room. Upon watching the bustling lobby, where there were more people than

rooms, he asked the owner about his business. The owner acknowledged his business was healthy, but what he really wanted to do was to try his hand in the oil business. After talking for a little while and checking the hotel's financials, Conrad offered to buy it. By the end of the day, Conrad Hilton was the proud owner of his first hotel.

(E) *How to use this story with an EXECUTIVE*

Executives are motivated by *Proof.* They want to win. Do the benefits of your product or services help them win? As you ask these questions and others, make sure the answer is you or your product.

- Do you have what you need to succeed?
- Are you aiming to own a "bank" when in reality you should be looking at "hotels?"
- What is the #1 challenge you have in business right now?

## P.I.C.K.S—Identify Needs: You Get 100 Percent of What You Don't Ask For

What is the value of a question? In Gary Keller's book, *The One Thing*, he said, "Answers come from questions, and the quality of any answer is directly determined by the quality of the question. Ask the wrong question, get the wrong answer. Ask the right question, get the right answer. Ask the most powerful question possible, and the answer can be life-altering."

The hot Florida sun was beating down on the university football players as they came off the field. Another humid, exhausting day. The typical player loses ten pounds during a game even though the coaches provide water. It was 1965; Dwayne Douglas, assistant football coach, asked what would seem like a simple question; however, it changed how sports were played forever. He asked Dr. Robert Cade, kidney disease specialist at the university, why his football players were losing up to fourteen pounds and not urinating after games.

They were drinking water but still losing weight. This simple question stumped the doctors. Through months of research they found that players were dehydrated.

It was the 1967 Orange Bowl, and the Florida Gators were facing the favorite, Georgia Tech. It was the Gators' first-ever Orange Bowl. In the first quarter, Georgia Tech took the lead, and it seemed like nothing the Gators were trying was working. They were getting destroyed. The Gators had used up so much energy early in the game that they had nothing left for the second half. The team doctors gave the players their drink of carbohydrates and electrolytes that would work quickly in their system and provide much-needed energy.

According to head football coach Ray Graves, "Whatever these guys came up with worked, because when the Gators came out the second half, they were a different team." As the other team seemed to tire, the Gators kept going, including one record-setting ninety-four-yard touchdown run. The Gators won that Orange Bowl. After the game, the coach for Georgia Tech, Bobby Dodd, told Graves, "We didn't have your drink. That made all the difference."

What is the value of a question? The doctors at the University of Florida named their sports drink after the football team's mascot, calling it Gatorade. In 1983, the doctors sold Gatorade for $220 million to the Quaker company. In 2001, Pepsi purchased Quaker and Gatorade for $13 billion. Today Gatorade does over $3.5 billion in sales annually. It is the official drink of seventy division-1 colleges as well as the NFL, NBA, MLB, and the PGA.

If you want to change your business or increase your sales, you need to be asking thought-provoking questions. These questions, if answered, would give you a connection with your customers. To use P.I.C.K.S. you need to Identify their needs based on their DRIVE. Here are lists of questions to dive deeper into what motivates them so you can unlock that final sale.

## (D) *Director Questions*

- Does your current job give you the lifestyle you desire?
- What would have to change in your life for you to have more freedom?
- Are you currently living your ideal life? If not, WHY?

## (R) *Relator Questions*

- Do you have the support you need to be successful?
- Do you want to be part of a community that will help you succeed?
- What do you want your legacy to be?

## (I) *Intellectual Questions*

- What is the ideal system you would want to use to be successful?
- What information do you feel you are missing to make the next decision?
- Do you currently have the system you need to succeed?

### *Validator Questions* (V)

- Do you feel trusted and respected in your current position?
- Are you being paid what you are worth?
- Does your current boss or situation validate all you do?

### *Executive Questions* (E)

- Are you winning and in control of your current situation?
- What would need to change in your life for you to be able to reach your goals?
- Do you feel you are on track to having the financial security you desire?

## P.I.C.K.S.—Call To Action: Asking Leads to Take Action

On June 30, 1859, Jean Francois Gravelot, better known as the Great Blondin, became the first person to cross Niagara Falls on a tight rope. It was a death-defying act, 160 feet above the river. That year he would do it eight different times. Each time the crowds would grow larger and larger.

One time, in front of 25,000 people, he asked the audience if they believed he could cross the tight rope using stilts. They all shouted, "We believe, we believe!" He proceeded to cross using just stilts.

Another time he asked the audience if they believed he could balance a chair on the tight rope and sit atop the chair. They shouted, "We believe, we believe!" And so, he did.

A few months later, he asked the raging crowd if they believed he could push a wheelbarrow across, and again they erupted, "We believe, we believe!" He then pushed the wheelbarrow across and asked, "Who believes I can put a person in the wheelbarrow and push them across?" The crowd of 100,000 exploded in cheers chanting, "We believe, we believe!"

Then the Great Blondin said, "Which one of you will get in the wheelbarrow?" The crowd went silent.

His manager, Harry Colcord, said he would not get in the wheelbarrow but would let the Great Blondin carry him on his back across the tight rope. On August 14th, in front of a hundred thousand people, Blondin crossed Niagara Falls with Harry on his back. The newspapers on the other side asked Harry why he would do such a thing. He was not under contract; there was no obligation for him to do so. He replied, "I have watched his discipline, I know his work ethic and his commitment to his craft. I knew he would not drop me."

A client I have worked with for years called me the other day and said, "I do not know why, but DRIVE does not work for me." Curious, I started to ask questions. He had a lifelong friend who he was selling, and his friend was following all the DRIVE questions. Everything seemed like it was working perfectly. However, his friend was not buying.

I finally asked him, "Did you ask for the sale?"

After a very long pause, he replied, "No, I guess I haven't."

Believe it or not, a lot of salespeople do not ask for the sale. They will ask clients to attend events, mixers, or networking socials but never actually ask for the sale. ASK FOR IT. If you have and they have said no and you have not been able to create a Reassociation, then ask them to make a small commitment.

Psychologists Jonathan Freedman and Scott Fraser did an experiment in Southern California where they asked homeowners to put a large sign in their yard that said, "Drive Carefully." Only seventeen percent said yes. With another group they asked if they could put a small three-inch sign that said, "Be A Safe Driver." Two weeks later they came back and asked those same people about putting in a large sign. An astonishing seventy-six percent said yes. A 450 percent increase. Small commitments lead to larger commitments.

If you are using P.I.C.K.S. to unlock the sale after you have gotten resistance, then ask your potential client to do something small like reading your white paper, or watch a short webinar, or attend one of your events.

For example, if you were inviting them to an event, you could say the following:

> **Director:** If I could show you a way to achieve your life's purpose and feel free and independent as you live the lifestyle you want through (insert your product or service) would that be worth thirty minutes of your time?
>
> **Relator:** If I could show you a way to support your most important and valued relationships and engage with a community of (insert your product or service) who are extremely focused on having a family mindset, would that be worth thirty minutes of your time?
>
> **Intellectual:** If I could help you access a proven system that would give you the knowledge you need to succeed in (insert your product or service), as well as step-by-step instructions on how to move forward, would that be worth thirty minutes of your time?
>
> **Validator:** If I could show you how to recognize your strengths, trust your ability to make a difference, and continue to be an

example people want to follow through (insert your product or service), would that be worth thirty minutes of your time?

**Executive:** If I could show you how to achieve your goals, solve problems and provide at a higher level through (insert your product or service), would that be worth thirty minutes of your time?

After they say yes to your small commitment, then you can have them commit to something bigger. Make sure when you talk to them or give them something, it adds real value. Create a Reassociation for them so they will want to commit to something larger.

## P.I.C.K.S.—Keep in Touch: Success is in the Follow Up

In 1962, Joe Girard filed for bankruptcy and closed his business. The bills continued to pile up. Eventually, the foreclosure notice was posted on his home. With no car, no groceries, and no money he found it impossible to provide for his wife and two children. Stressed out, he

[©Joe Girard]

boarded the bus to Detroit looking for work. The doors opened in front of a Chevrolet dealership. Without hesitation, he walked up to the manager and begged for a job. The manager had mercy and gave him an opportunity on a trial basis. Girard spent the entire day calling everyone he knew to see if anyone needed a new car. By 8:30 p.m. he exhausted all his contacts. The other salesmen had gone home, but Girard decided to stay till closing. Fortunately, a customer walked up while another salesman was preoccupied. He spent ninety minutes answering every question and did a little more begging and by the end of the night he sold his first car.

With no money in his pocket, he borrowed ten bucks from his manager to buy bus fare and groceries for his family. The next month he sold eighteen cars. The salesmen complained to the manager that Girard was taking all their sales, and he was swiftly fired. He went to Merollis Chevrolet in suburban Detroit and started to set sales records year after year.

Girard went on to become the greatest car salesman in history, selling 13,001 cars in fifteen years. From 1966 through 1977, Girard won the annual title as the world's number one car salesman, according to the *Guinness Book of World Records*. What was his secret? Keeping In Touch. In addition to giving top-notch service to his clients, he kept in touch and remembered important occasions like birthdays and anniversaries and sent random holiday cards like St. Patrick's Day, July 4th, and those obscure holidays no one else acknowledges. "Joe sent out nearly 13,000 greeting cards a month to his customers, celebrating everything from Halloween to Groundhog's Day," according to the *Detroit News*.

Whatever happened to his original boss who fired him? Don't worry, he kept in touch with him as well. Every year he mailed a copy of his W-2 to his old boss, with a note at the bottom telling him, "You fired the wrong guy." After his old boss died, Girard says he even took a W-2 to the cemetery and buried it atop the man's casket.

"I never sold a car in my life," Girard said. "I sold a Girard." You are not selling a product or service; you are selling yourself.

Following up is where you will find success because others fail to Keep In Touch. Herbert True, a marketing specialist at Notre Dame, found that most people quit asking for the sale after the first couple of contacts:

- 44 percent of all salespeople quit after the first call
- 24 percent quit after the second call
- 14 percent quit after the third call
- 12 percent quit trying to sell their prospect after the fourth call

This means ninety-four percent of all salespeople quit after the fourth call. But sixty percent of all sales are made on the fifth call. This means ninety-four percent of all salespeople miss out on sixty percent of all sales. It also means six percent of the top earners are getting sixty percent of all sales.

When reaching out to your potential customer, customize your emails, texts, social media posts, or letters in a way that will engage their DRIVE:

### D *Director*

- Create a correspondence that enhances their lifestyle.
- Create a correspondence that gives them a clear vision of financial and time freedom.
- Create a correspondence that is a VIP experience.

### R *Relator*

- Create a correspondence that connects them to the family or friends.
- Create a correspondence that builds and uplifts their community.
- Create a correspondence that will help them give back.

**Intellectual** (I)

- Create a correspondence with step-by-step actions to succeed.
- Create a correspondence that asks for their opinion.
- Create a correspondence that will highlight their intelligence.

**Validator** (V)

- Create a correspondence that describes their future success.
- Create a correspondence that compliments the time you have spent with them.
- Create a correspondence that highlights their accomplishments.

**Executive** (E)

- Create a correspondence that provides proof that it works.
- Create a correspondence that provides third-party testimonials.
- Create a correspondence that focuses on the big picture.

## P.I.C.K.S.—Surprise Them: Surprise is the Highest Level of Engagement

My phone rang. "Hi, this is Stephanie. Who are you and why do I have flowers on my desk?"

"Thank you for calling me," I replied. "We are going to change the world with this movie, and I need your help to make it happen."

When I was filming my first movie (*i-ology*), I needed over 250 clips of High Definition (HD) stock footage. The average price per clip at the time was about $900. After researching the best company in the industry, I called the secretary and asked for the person in charge of stock footage. Upon getting her name, I called 1-800-FLOWERS and sent her a basket of flowers with a note that said, "Thank you in advance for helping me with my movie project. Sincerely, Woody (XXX) XXX-XXXX."

I received that phone call from Stephanie within three days. I went on to tell her how I needed her company to donate stock footage for my movie that was going to change the world. She said, "No, we are a business. We sell stock footage for a living." She instructed me it was impossible; the company would not donate the required footage. I tried every *ASK. Don't Tell* technique I could think of.

After about fifteen minutes of getting told "no," she finally said, "If you will send me your script, distribution plan, shooting dates, and locations, I will take it to my boss. Call us back in thirty days and we can discuss it."

"I will have it all to you in forty-eight hours," I replied. I didn't have anything she asked for, so it was a very long forty-eight hours trying to make it all up. At day fifteen, I sent both Stephanie and her boss movie passes, a box of popcorn with candies, and a note saying, "Enjoy a movie on me." On day twenty-nine, I sent a box of chocolates and another note saying, "Thank you in advance for helping make my movie."

When the time arrived for our conference call, both Stephanie and her boss were grateful for the gifts but said, "Woody, as you know we are a business and we cannot give you the number of clips you want for free. What we are willing to do is sell you as many clips as you need for $50 apiece. Would that work for you?"

I had spent roughly $257.83 on their gifts and now I was saving over $200,000 for stock footage. I was sure they could hear me smiling when I said, "Would you like a credit card or wire transfer?"

Why did such a crazy approach work? Dr. David Schwartz said, "Man's most compelling non-biological hunger is to feel important." When we make others feel important, it changes the way we do business.

When a sale starts to go stagnant it is usually because your prospect has disengaged. Gallup Poll Research interviewed twenty-five million employees in 197 countries with seventy languages and found seventy percent of all employees are not engaged. This disengagement is costing the United States an estimated $450 billion to $550 billion annually. According to the report:

> The moment an employee connects emotionally with a customer is a source of untapped power that has profound implications for a company's productivity and profitability. When organizations know how to prepare front-line employees to make the most of these moments, they engage customers—who in turn spend more, visit more often, resist competitive overtures, promote their brand to others, and forgive the occasional service blunder. When organizations successfully engage their customers and their employees, they experience a 240 percent boost in performance-related business outcomes."

A dear friend of mine, Levi McPherson, and I were sitting around over lunch one day. We wondered if we could combine our business expertise and create a product from scratch and within thirty days do six figures in sales. To accomplish this outlandish idea, we knew we would have to engage our potential customers. To do so, we outlined the five principles of the Law of Engagement. As you apply these in your business you will see people engage and buy more.

## The Laws of Engagement

### *Five Principles to Profitable Engagement*

1. We Are Always Engaged In Something
2. Anticipation Enhances Engagement
3. Engagement Is Equal To Delivery
4. Surprise Is The Highest Level Of Engagement
5. Sustainable Engagement Happens Through Repetition With Variation

*On the 29th day after we launched, our new venture cleared six figures within twenty-four hours.

*Principle #1: We Are Always Engaged In Something*

Today more than ever people are constantly distracted by their phones, binge-watching shows, or checking social media. Does your message break through the noise? Do you have a grabber in your marketing message to get their attention? What can you implement that will get their attention?

Solution: Make Some Noise Based On What Would Engage Their DRIVE

- What is your grabber?
- Shocking stunt (Pepsi Challenge)
- Unique and original press release—disrupt their thinking patterns

*Principle #2: Anticipation Enhances Engagement*

The day before a trip, Black Friday, Cyber Monday, the night before your wedding, or the day before your favorite team is in the playoffs are moments when you are completely engaged because you are anticipating something favorable will happen. Are you creating anticipation with your clients by releasing the 2.0 version of your product? Is there a discount or sale you could do that would increase anticipation? As you create anticipation your clients become more engaged.

Solution: Build Anticipation Based On Their DRIVE

- Invite a guest speaker
- What exclusive promise can you give?
- Free gift

*Principle #3: Engagement Is Equal To Delivery*

Who makes more money: Disneyland or the state fair? Disneyland of course. Their delivery from the clean streets to unique rides to themed restaurants to costumed characters makes you feel engaged versus your state fair that has a unique smell, rides that feel like they are going to break, and the food that makes you sick for days. What is the delivery of your product? Think about your packaging. What is the customer's experience? How does your customer's experience affect their five senses (touch, taste, smell, sight, and hearing)?

Solution: Deliver More Than You Promise To Engage Their DRIVE

- Environment
- Experiences
- Five Senses

*Principle #4: Surprise Is The Highest Level Of Engagement*

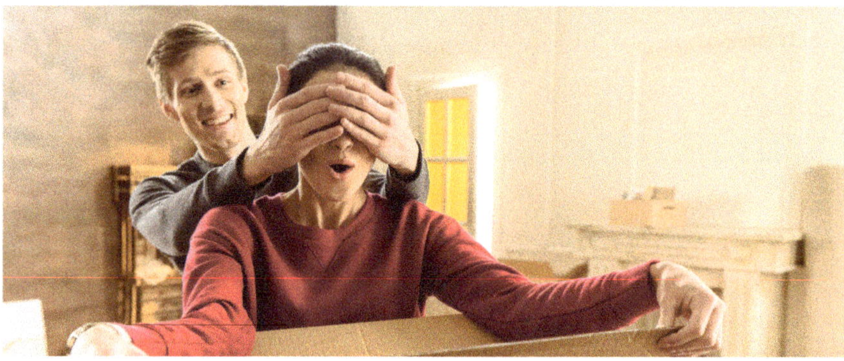

What is the most engaging ten seconds you have ever experienced? Having asked this question for years the top answers have been "near-death experience," "sex," or "seeing my baby born." These have a surprise built into them. When was the last time you were surprised? Was it an unexpected raise or tax refund? Maybe a surprise party? When is the last time you had a first time? This year we were in Paris and decided to visit Disneyland Paris. As we walked the streets in awe my wife said, "When was the last time you got to go to Disneyland for the first time?" We used to live in Southern California and would go to Disneyland every Monday at 3:30 p.m. Our family has been to the Magic Kingdom more times than I care to admit. But being in a different country and seeing Disneyland Paris as an adult felt like a complete surprise. When was the last time you surprised your clients? If you want to use P.I.C.K.S. to unlock opportunities, Surprise Them.

Solution: Create Shock And Awe Specific To Their DRIVE

- Customized gifts
- Unexpected sale
- VIP experience

*Principle #5: Sustainable Engagement Happens Through Repetition With Variation*

© Frank Heinz / Alamy Stock Photo

What do Nike, Taco Bell, and Absolut Vodka have to do with your success? They are incredible brands that have a very repetitious product but with a little variation that makes you feel it is fresh and new. Nike has had the same slogan "Just Do It" for decades. It is very repetitious, but where they make a variation is in the athletes they sponsor. A shoe ad is a shoe ad, but when you have a Michael Jordan, Kobe Bryant, or Lebron James in a Nike shoe ad it feels fresh.

Think about Taco Bell. It seems like they only have five ingredients but those five make fifty menu items. There is a tortilla, beans, cheese, rice, and meat but when you roll it, grill it, flatten it, deep fry it, or fold it, you get a new product.

Absolut Vodka made its bottle the most recognizable bottle in the world. Its campaign, which featured print ads showing bottles "in the wild," was so successful that they didn't stop running it for twenty-five years. It's the longest uninterrupted ad campaign ever and comprises over 1,500 separate ads. Same bottle, different variation. This one technique took them from only 2.5 percent to 50 percent market share.

If your product or pitch seems mundane, then you need to spice it up with a little variation.

Solution: Make It Fresh And New To Engage Their DRIVE

- Packaging redesign
- New slogan
- New sponsors

As you use the five laws of engagement, apply them to each DRIVE for a greater response.

### D Director: *How does your product or services help them . . .*

- Experience Life
- Achieve their Life's Purpose
- Be Free and Independent
- Express their Creativity
- Perform as they choose
- Overcome Challenges
- Feel confident with their Appearance

### R Relator: *How does your product or services help them . . .*

- Build healthy Relationships
- Have a power of Influence
- Give service and Volunteer
- Support their Family
- Connect with Friends
- Be a good Parent
- Connect with God, Spirit, or the Universe as defined by them

### I Intellectual: *How does your product or services help them . . .*

- Rely on their Knowledge
- Learn something new
- Live and feel Healthy
- Connect to Nature
- Be in the Moment
- Honor their Standards
- Be more Organized

**Validator: How does your product or services help them . . .** (V)

- Give or receive Recognition
- Give or receive Acceptance
- Give or receive Praise
- Give or receive Trust
- Give or receive Respect
- Give or receive Validation

**Executive: How does your product or services help them . . .** (E)

- Feel like they are Winning
- Have a sense of Control
- Have success in their Work
- Reach their Goals
- Feel a sense of Security
- Provide for the people they choose
- Solve problems

Congratulations on finishing the book. Here are the next steps to increasing your sales.

## DRIVE Sales Process

**Step 1:** First Contact—Get To Know Them: Use the DRIVE Cards/Handout or the Conversation Close.

**Step 2:** Solve Their Problems Based On Their DRIVE. Create Buying Behavior Through Reassociations.

- ASK. Don't Tell.
- SHOW. Don't Tell.
- Ask For The Sale.

**Step 3:** Use P.I.C.K.S. To Resolve Concerns

SPECIAL
BONUS
SPECIAL

# Bonus Case Studies

## DRIVE Sales Through Borrowing An Audience

Having trained salespeople for over twenty years, I want to give you my foolproof, seven-figure secret strategy I have personally used to build my business. As entrepreneurs and salespeople, we are constantly trying to find our treasure. When seeking your treasure, you will use many different maps. In business, the acronym for M.A.P.S. is as follows. You can divide companies into three different categories: they are either a Message, Products, or Service company. They can be one of the three or a combination of the three.

Apple, for example, is a Products and Service company. They sell hardware through their iPhones, iPads, and computers. They are also a service company through the iTunes store. Tom's Shoes is a Message and Products business. Their message is in their brand: buy one, give one. When you buy a pair of their shoes, they give a pair to someone in need. Is your company a Message, Products, or Service company?

When trying to find your treasure on the map, you need to know where the X is located. In this analogy, X is the multiplier. What you are missing in M.A.P.S. is the A, which stands for Audience. To find your treasure you need to find your audience.

*The equation for success is M.P.S. x A = $$$.*

Take Oprah Winfrey for example. When she was at the height of her TV show, she had an audience of millions of viewers that generated a billion-dollar net worth. If you look at a school teacher who has an audience of thirty kids, their annual income will cap out around $60,000 a year. It doesn't mean their Product, Service, or Message is any less valuable. Their income is directly tied to the size of their audience. If you take away the A from MAPS, all you have left is PMS and you're anxious, crabby, and angry. To avoid the frustration, there are actually three ways to obtain your audience: Buy, Build, or Borrow.

**Buy:** Traditionally, people would buy their audiences through purchasing spots on the radio, billboards, newsprint, or magazines, then later, Google AdWords and Facebook. This can be very costly with no guaranteed result.

**Build:** Building an audience requires an enormous amount of time. According to most audience building professionals, it will take a minimum of one to two years of posting, blogging, creating videos, and constantly fighting to stay relevant. This takes a long time and an enormous commitment.

**Borrow:** This is the third and best way to build your empire. Before I was forty years old, I had built four multi-million dollar companies in completely different industries. The only way I was able to do this was to borrow an audience. When Thomas Edison needed an audience for his batteries, he created a joint venture (JV) with Henry Ford and his vehicles. When Henry Ford needed tires for his Model A, he turned to Harvey Firestone and created a mutual JV.

The best way to create a JV is to identify someone who has an audience (A) that would benefit from your product, service, or message (M.P.S.). The recipe for success is M.P.S. x A = $$$. In the previous chapters, you have already identified your products, advantages, and solutions with regards to the challenges of each DRIVE. After you have identified someone who has an audience that would benefit from your M.P.S., you can then create value for them personally. The easiest way is to solve a problem for them. I find the fastest way to become indispensable to a new relationship is to solve one of their biggest problems they are dealing with. Remember, you are compensated in direct proportion to the problems you solve. After you have solved a problem then you can introduce your Message, Product, or Service to their Audience.

One of the best examples of this process is Dean Kamen, inventor of the Segway and 440 other patents. He had come up with a new idea to purify water for third-world countries where 3.5 million people die annually because of diseases resulting from the consumption of unsanitary water. His new technology, the Slingshot, can transform ninety-seven percent of undrinkable water into water that can be used and consumed on the spot, readily and inexpensively.

The device takes contaminated water and runs it through a vapor-compression distiller producing 250 gallons of clean water daily, enough for 100 people. The devices have been used with "anything that looks wet," including polluted river water, saline ocean water, and raw sewage. His product literally saves lives. Kamen met with government officials and dignitaries around the world, and no one would help him get his product into villages. He personally met with the United Nations (who represent 130 countries) but was turned down and told they could not help him.

Then he reached out to the CEO of the Coca Cola Company with the idea to create clean water. Coke is in over 200 countries, and their biggest challenge at the time was finding clean water to make their soda in India and in other contaminated territories. At one point, Coke had to stop selling in India because they could not find a source of clean water.

This is one of the largest markets with over 1.2 billion potential customers. Another problem Coke faced was their need to redesign the soda fountain, something that had not changed in over sixty years. Coke's then CEO, Muhtar Kent, told Kamen if he could help them

create a new soda fountain, they would help him get his purifiers into countries around the world. Kamen and his team spent two years designing and redesigning what became the new Coke Freestyle machine.

The Freestyle machine was an instant success. A standard soda dispenser can usually only deliver six to eight options. The Freestyle dispenser has over a hundred. By Kamen solving their problems, he was introduced to an unlimited audience of people who need his lifesaving Slingshot machine.

On a more local level and something that is more applicable to you and I is a client of mine, Nate Lambert. For two years he ranked #5 in a large direct selling company. All of a sudden I saw his numbers shoot through the roof netting a six-figure income in one month and then the next month. I was getting on a flight when I called him and asked him what the difference had been. He said, "Woody, you taught me four years ago to borrow an audience. I finally implemented it and I saw my sales skyrocket." By the end of the year he was the #1 income earner out of thousands of salespeople.

Example of industries that have an audience:

- Lawyers
- Financial Planners
- Insurance Salesmen
- Tax Advisors
- Realtors
- Influencers
- Mortgage Brokers
- Business Owners
- Network Marketers
- Commission Salespeople

Here are the steps to creating a mutual joint venture:

1. Identify who has an audience that would benefit from your Message, Product, or Service.
2. Create value by solving the problem of the influencer over that audience.
3. Discover the influencer's DRIVE so you know how to customize your solutions.
4. After you have solved the problem then show the influencer how bringing your Message, Product, or Service to his/her audience will be hugely beneficial.
5. Follow up, create value by solving problems, rinse and repeat.

## Decorating With DRIVE To Increase Sales

The reason why I wrote about Bruce Halle was while I was sitting in Discount Tire's lobby, I looked up on the waiting room wall and saw five independent posters that screamed DRIVE. It made me curious about Discount, its founder, and their marketing.

One poster says, "STREET STYLE" with a picture of a car and five different custom wheel samples with the tagline, "The world's largest selection of custom wheels." This appeals to the Director's desire for customization, creativity, uniqueness, and individuality. The next one was, "Americas' Neighborhood Tire Store since 1960." The poster is covered with images of different races in different communities around the United States. This appeals to the Relator's desire to be inclusive and supportive of community. The following poster appeals to Intellectuals talking about their "Certificate for Repair, Refund, or Replacement." This addresses the step-by-step process and the important information that would appeal to an Intellectual. The next read, "Our Promise To You. Providing an Inviting, Easy, & Safe Experience" with two hands from different races creating an image of unity. It will appeal to a Validator's desire for respect, trust, and acceptance. Lastly,

the remaining poster says, "Winning Team" with Discount Tires three NASCAR drivers and the car racing on the track. This obviously appeals to an Executive's desire to win.

Another client of mine, Richard Stock, has five posters he created around DRIVE in his presentation room. When he is doing his seminars he will point to the wall and say, "Looking at those posters—which one do you resonate with?" This helps him prime his audience to recognize what they really want. In his personal office, when he is closing people he has the same five posters but smaller, and he ask the same questions. Quickly he will know their DRIVE and then customize his pitch accordingly.

As we have seen with Buy-ology, subconscious imagery can help your potential customers connect their DRIVE with your place of business.

## DRIVE in Pop Culture

As I pulled my car into the underground valet in Beverly Hills, I knew that this was going to be a different type of meeting. I was ushered through the private barbershop to a set of elevators that took me to an executive suite. My PR agent at the time set up the appointment with this Hollywood producer working on a new project. He was stuck on character development. As I sat down, he told me he had been following my work and reached out to my agent and requested an introduction.

For the next eight hours we went through each character's DRIVE and what motivated them, how they would show up in different scenarios, and how they would respond in any circumstance. This gave the producer the ammunition he needed to develop the project into another success.

Films and television collectively generate roughly $300 billion in revenue each year. When you analyze the sales cycle of the entertainment industry it is by far one of the most challenging. Living near L.A. for ten years, I have clients and friends in Hollywood who live and die with show acceptance or cancellations.

When you sit down to binge-watch your favorite series, what you may not know is it takes on average two to three years before the show hits the air. You have to craft a thirty to ninety second pitch to get a producer's attention. If you are fortunate enough to succeed in this, then you pitch the studio. There are countless months of back and forth negotiations with a studio for a green light. If you are successful at getting their attention and raise the necessary capital, then you have months of development and filming a pilot.

Even with a pilot you are not out of the woods yet. There is casting, wardrobe, hiring a director, sound, lighting, cinematography, editing, commercial space to sell, production, writing and rewriting until you begin to question your very existence for being in the industry. If you are lucky, after the pilot you get picked up for a season. Even after your first season you are not safe; only twenty percent of shows get picked up for a second season.

Of the thousands of shows on TV or being streamed, in the last twenty years there have been less than fifteen TV shows to be awarded nine or more seasons. To be in the top 0.1 percent of TV is no small feat. To be bold, I believe it is because the writers represented each of the five DRIVE personalities. It has to be something more than they got lucky or it just resonated with the right generation. If that was the case, Netflix would not have paid a $100 million to stream *Friends* for the 2019 season.

Netflix's most popular streaming show is *The Office.* Spending more hours than I care to admit binge-watching these shows for this research, I want to illustrate what I have found. If you analyze the characters and the five DRIVE personalities, you can clearly see them represented. If this works for a $300-billion industry to get the shows into the highest tier, imagine what it could do for your business.

*The Office* is a unique example because we have two versions of the show to compare how DRIVE affects its success and longevity. The UK version only had one season with 14 episodes while the US version had 209 episodes during its nine seasons. According to Screen Rant, you can see how they were developed differently.

> For the most part, both the UK and America's versions of *The Office* have an equal amount of characters, but you'll notice that America's supporting cast is much more well-developed. Why is that? Probably because Ryan "The Temp" (B.J. Novak), Kelly Kapoor (Mindy Kaling) and Toby from H.R. (Paul Lieberstein) also double as chief writers for the show. When your supporting characters are writing countless episodes for the series, it's inevitable that they're going to expand the depth of supporting cast members.

Novak, Kaling and Lieberstein were able to tap into DRIVE because of their experience as both a writer and an actor on the show. This kept the authenticity of true character development in each episode.

- **Director:** Jim Halpert and Darryl Philbin
  - Jim is free-spirited, spontaneous, and loves to fill his day doing pranks on Dwight. He doesn't take things too seriously. He just wants to be free and have fun. "Right now, this is just a job. If I advance any higher in this company, this would be my career. And, uh, if this were my career, I'd have to throw myself in front of a train." —Jim Halpert
  - Darryl does not respect Michael's authority when he comes into the warehouse. He jumps at the opportunity to take off and start a new business with Jim. He can take or leave his relationship with Kelly. When Kelly pressures him to know where their relationship is going, he says, "I like you, but you need to access your un-crazy side; otherwise, maybe this thing has run its course." —Darryl Philbin

- **Relator:** Pam Beesly, Phyllis Vance
  - Pam is all about her community. She is loyal in her relationships and tries to include everyone. When referring to her relationship with Jim and her family she said, "When you're a kid, you assume your parents are soul mates. My kids are going to be right about that." —Pam Beesly
  - Phyllis wants to oversee the planning committee so she can include more people. She loves to show off her relationship with Bob Vance from Vance Refrigeration. "Well, I just think we all deserve to be with someone who wants to be with us." —Phyllis Vance
- **Intellectual:** Angela Martin, Stanley Hudson, Oscar Martinez
  - Angela does not like change. She wants to stay on a schedule. She's organized and thorough. She feels that everyone else is not doing their job properly. "I don't want to blame anyone in particular. I think everyone's to blame." —Angela Martin
  - Stanley sits doing his crossword puzzles, ignoring everyone else because he does not want to be bothered unless it is work-related. "I would rather work for an upturned broom with a bucket for a head than work for somebody else in this office besides myself." —Stanley Hudson
  - Oscar likes to butt himself into every conversation by saying, "actually. . ." and then inserting some interesting fact. In Season 7, Episode 10, Michael happens to get something right about China and Oscar corrects him even though he is wrong. When Kelly teases him about Michael being correct Oscar says distastefully, "He's not smarter than me. He was just right about one thing." —Oscar Martinez
- **Validator:** Michael Scott, Andy Bernard, Kelly Kapoor
  - Michael is great at validating others with the Dundies Awards, wants to make everyone happy, and is not as productive if he feels people don't like him. "Would I rather be feared or loved?

Easy. Both. I want people to be afraid of how much they love me." —Michael Scott

- Andy loves to talk about how he went to an Ivy League school, Cornell, even though he is just selling paper. He relishes how important he was in his acapella group. He tries to get everyone to love him. In Season 3, Episode 8, the Merger, he said, "I'll be the number-two guy here in Scranton in six weeks. How? Name repetition, personality mirroring, and never breaking off a handshake." —Andy Bernard
- Kelly tries to get everyone's attention. She showed up at Phyllis's wedding in a white dress. To keep Ryan's attention, she tells him she is pregnant when he wanted to breakup. When she asked what her New Year's resolutions were she said, "My resolution is to get more attention." —Kelly Kapoor

- **Executive:** Ryan Howard, Dwight Schrute
  - Ryan goes to business school so he can win and no longer be a temp. He takes control when he gets a promotion to be Michael's boss. He only wants Kelly when she is with someone else. He wants to take control and win. "I am keeping a list of everyone who wrongs me so when I am back on top they will be sorry." —Ryan Howard
  - Dwight wants to have complete control over the office, including Michael's job. He wants to win Angela from Andy. To be in control, he buys the building and becomes the landlord for Dunder Mifflin. "Nothing stresses me out. Except having to seek the approval of my inferiors." —Dwight Schrute

## F·R·I·E·N·D·S—*Ten Seasons*

- **Director:** Phoebe Buffay
  - Phoebe is creative, free-spirited, enjoys playing her guitar her way, and lives her life by her terms.

- **Relator:** Chandler Bing
  - Chandler did have commitment issues but stayed loyal to Monica. He is loyal to his friends as well.
- **Intellectual:** Ross Geller
  - Ross does not like to be challenged intellectually. He loves to share what he knows with others—even if they are bored.
- **Validator:** Joey Tribbiani and Rachel Green
  - Joey and Rachel want to be admired and respected at work and amongst their friends. They do not like to be ignored. They are great at supporting others.
- **Executive:** Monica Geller
  - Monica is a bit of a control freak. She likes to win too, and can get really intense and competitive.

## the BIG BANG THEORY—*Twelve Seasons*

- **Director:** Penny Hofstadter and Howard Wolowitz
  - Penny is an extrovert. She is very social and has a laid-back attitude. She is up for anything fun and exciting.
  - Howard is the most adventurous of the four male leads. He brags about his escapades with women (which he probably did not have). He is open to new possibilities.
- **Relator:** Amy Farrah Fowler and Leonard Hofstadter
  - Amy wants nothing more than a relationship with her equal, Sheldon. She strives to like Penny even though Penny is nowhere near her intellect.
  - Leonard works hard to make Penny happy. Relationships with his friends mean the world to him. Though he is smart he is humble and lets his colleagues take the spotlight.

- **Intellectual:** Sheldon Cooper
    - Sheldon is always right. He creates a system for his relationships by creating roommate and girlfriend contracts. He believes he is the smartest in the group.
- **Validator:** Raj Koothrappali
    - Raj has had a tough time with the ladies and is gun shy of putting himself out there. He supports and lifts his friends. Occasionally, when he has not had attention for a while, he will be sarcastic.
- **Executive:** Bernadette Rostenkowski
    - Bernadette is a fireball of power and authority. When she wants something, she makes it happen. She holds people accountable.

When you analyze the top movie franchises with an ensemble cast you can see the same pattern with DRIVE.

Harry Potter: *eight movies, $7.7 billion in box office receipts*

- **Director:** Fred and George Weasley
- **Relator:** Harry Potter
- **Intellectual:** Hermione Granger
- **Validator:** Ron Weasley
- **Executive:** Draco Malfoy

Avengers: *four movies, $7.6 billion in box office receipts*

- **Director:** Iron Man
- **Relator:** Captain America, Black Widow
- **Intellectual:** Bruce Banner, Dr. Strange
- **Validator:** Loki, Hulk
- **Executive:** Thor, Thanos, Hawkeye

## STAR WARS: *eight movies, $7.4 billion in box office receipts*

- **Director:** Luke Skywalker
- **Relator:** Princess Leia, Chewbacca
- **Intellectual:** C-3PO
- **Validator:** Han Solo
- **Executive:** Darth Vader

## FAST & FURIOUS: *eight movies, $5.4 billion in box office receipts*

- **Director:** Brian O'Connor
- **Relator:** Domini Toretto, Mia Toretto
- **Intellectual:** Tej Parker, Han
- **Validator:** Roman Pearce
- **Executive:** Letty, Luke Hobbs

An interesting side note is that when *Fast and the Furious* changed their characters in the third film, *Tokyo Drift,* it disrupted the DRIVE. It was the least profitable film in the series. Other than #3, each new movie increased in worldwide sales, which is unheard of for a movie franchise. Number 7 had an extra pump because Paul Walker who plays Brian O'Connor passed away in real life.

| | Title | Worldwide Sales |
|---|---|---|
| 1 | *The Fast and the Furious* | $ 207,283,925.00 |
| 2 | *2 Fast 2 Furious* | $ 236,350,661.00 |
| 3 | *The Fast and the Furious: Tokyo Drift* | $ 158,468,292.00 |
| 4 | *Fast and Furious* | $ 363,164,265.00 |
| 5 | *Fast Five* | $ 626,137,675.00 |
| 6 | *Fast and Furious 6* | $ 788,679,850.00 |
| 7 | *Furious 7* | $ 1,516,045,911.00 |
| 8 | *The Fate of the Furious* | $ 1,236,005,118.00 |
| | Total Worldwide Sales | $ 5,132,135,697.00 |

This is crucial to understand even if you are not planning on writing and selling a TV show or movie—you are writing a marketing piece, building out your pitch, delivering your pitch to a customer, asking for the sale, and resolving concerns to get them to buy. Your product is your TV show.

## This Is Not A Conclusion

Every editor I spoke with said, "Woody, you need to include a conclusion." Well, by now, you know I am a Director, and I am going to abide by my own rules. I am not adding a conclusion to the end of the book because you are at the beginning of your journey. Now that you understand DRIVE, you are aware that it isn't a one size fits all. There is no end. It has to be practiced every day, over and over again.

Walt Disney famously said that "Disneyland will never be completed. It will continue to grow as long as there is imagination left in the world." I feel the same way about DRIVE. As long as people are selling and sharing their products and services with the world, DRIVE will continue to develop and help those who need it.

Here is my personal email address: woody@DriveSalesBook.com. Write to me and let me know how you are using DRIVE to increase your sales, and what I might do to serve you. I would love to share your stories and successes with the world in my next book.

Do Good—Be Good.

CPSIA information can be obtained
at www.ICGtesting.com
Printed in the USA
BVHW061633140920
588791BV00001B/1/J

9 781735 331706